Glear

Volume 1

Extracts from the Letters of Samuel Rutherford

Selected by Hamilton Smith

Scripture Truth Publications

EXTRACTS FROM THE LETTERS OF SAMUEL RUTHERFORD

Hardback edition first published 1913 by The Central Bible Truth Depôt, 12 Paternoster Row, London, E.C.
Re-typeset and transferred to Digital Printing 2008
ISBN: 978-0-901860-81-1 (paperback)
© Copyright 1913 The Central Bible Truth Depôt and 2008 Scripture Truth

A publication of Scripture Truth

All rights reserved. No part of this publication may be reproduced, stored in a retrieval system, or transmitted, in any form or by any means, electronic, mechanical, photocopying, recording or otherwise without prior permission of Scripture Truth Publications.

Scripture quotations are taken from The Authorized (King James) Version. Rights in the Authorized Version are vested in the Crown. Reproduced by permission of the Crown's patentee, Cambridge University Press.

Verses are taken from "Last words of Reverend Samuel Rutherford: with some of his sweet sayings" (*The Christian Treasury*, 1857) by Mrs Anne Ross Cousin (1824-1906)
Cover photograph ©iStockphoto.com/iacon (Jeffery Borchert)

Published by Scripture Truth Publications
31-33 Glover Street, Crewe, Cheshire, CW1 3LD
Scripture Truth is an imprint of Central Bible Hammond Trust, a charitable trust

Typesetting by John Rice
Printed and bound by Lightning Source

EXTRACTS FROM THE LETTERS OF SAMUEL RUTHERFORD

Preface

"Alas! I see not what service I can do to Him, except it be to talk a little, and babble upon a piece of paper concerning the love of Christ."

Thus wrote Samuel Rutherford, from his prison, in 1637. For a period of seventeen months he was confined to the city of Aberdeen, inhibited from all public ministry. But though his lips were sealed, his heart was welling forth with "a good matter", and hence he acquired the pen of a ready writer.

The following extracts from his letters will enable the reader to test the quality of the babbling stream that flowed from his palace-prison to cheer the saints of God for well-nigh three hundred years. And if a draught at this refreshing stream makes Christ, and His love that passeth knowing, more real, and more precious to some thirsty soul, it will not be in vain that a poor prisoner of Christ once babbled, upon a piece of paper, concerning the love of Christ.

Hamilton Smith

1913

EXTRACTS FROM THE LETTERS OF SAMUEL RUTHERFORD

EXTRACTS FROM THE LETTERS OF SAMUEL RUTHERFORD

Contents

PAGE

PREFACE 3

BIOGRAPHICAL INTRODUCTION 7

CHAPTER

1. THE WORD OF WARNING 13
2. THE TROUBLED SOUL 21
3. THE WAY OF PEACE 26
4. THE PRESENT EVIL WORLD 31
5. THE FLESH AND THE DEVIL 37
6. "THE DAY OF AFFLICTION" 41
7. "THE FIERY TRIAL" 51
8. THE SHADOW OF DEATH 58
9. THE HOUSE OF MOURNING 61
10. THE WORD OF COMFORT 68
11. THE PILGRIM 74
12. THE ETERNAL WEIGHT OF GLORY 80
13. THE EXCELLENCIES OF CHRIST 87

EXTRACTS FROM THE LETTERS OF SAMUEL RUTHERFORD

Biographical Introduction

Samuel Rutherford may be regarded as Preacher, Controversialist, or Letter-writer. As *the Preacher*, he was homely, pithy, moving, and affectionate, appealing almost exclusively to the congregations of his day. As *the Controversialist*, he was the profound scholar, presenting his ecclesiastical convictions with all the religious fervour of his fiery nature; and as such he was, in a large degree, the servant of a party. As *the Letter-writer*, he was the heavenly-minded saint, appealing to the affections of God's people for all time.

Rutherford was born about the year 1600, in a village of Roxburghshire. Of his conversion no details have been recorded, save only, that he himself tells us, "Like a fool as I was, I suffered my sun to be high in the heavens, and near afternoon, before ever I took the gate." Probably it was about 1625, at the close of his brilliant college career, that he took the strait gate and the narrow way which leadeth unto life.

In 1627 he was settled at "fair Anwoth by the Solway", a land of secluded valleys and wooded hills. For nine years he ministered, as Preacher and Pastor, to a scattered and rural flock. His habit was to rise at three in the morning and commence his day alone with God in prayer and meditation. It was said of him, "He is *always* praying, *always* preaching, *always* visiting the sick, *always* catechising. *always* writing and studying." He is described by his contemporaries as a man who, whether walking or preaching, held "aye his face upward", as if he already saw the King in His beauty, and beheld the Land that is very far off. Little wonder that a hearer testified of his preaching, "He showed me the loveliness of Christ."

Such ministry, richly blessed to large congregations, could hardly escape the opposition of the Devil. In 1636 the storm burst. Rutherford's persistent refusal to conform to Episcopacy, and the publication of his work against Arminianism, made him highly obnoxious to the Ecclesiastical Authorities of the day. He was summoned before a High Commission Court at Wigtown, presided over by Sydserff, the intolerant Bishop of Galloway, and later before the Court at Edinburgh. By these Courts he was deposed from his ministerial office, forbidden to preach in any part of Scotland, and banished to Aberdeen to remain within the precincts of the city during the King's pleasure.

The opposition had apparently succeeded. In reality the devil had outwitted himself. True, the preaching of Christ, to limited congregations, was for the moment silenced, but only to give place to a ministry of Christ, that has been for the blessing and comfort of the generation of God's people for all the succeeding years. At first his "silent Sabbaths" weighed heavily upon his spirit. But the gloom passed, and so feasted was he with the love of Christ that he can write, "My prison is a palace to me, and Christ's banqueting house."

BIOGRAPHICAL INTRODUCTION

Of his three hundred and sixty-two letters that have been preserved, two hundred and nineteen were written during the seventeen months he was confined in "Christ's prison palace" of Aberdeen.

In 1638, taking advantage of the national rising against Episcopacy, Rutherford left his place of exile. For a short time he returned to his beloved Anwoth. In 1639 he reluctantly accepted the position of Professor of Divinity in the New College at St. Andrews University—making it a condition that he should be allowed to continue his preaching.

From November, 1643, until November, 1647, we find Rutherford residing in London, in attendance upon the Westminster Assembly, as one of the representatives of the Church of Scotland.

Returning to St. Andrews, he was appointed Principal of the New College, and, four years later, Rector of the University. During the years that followed, while zealously performing his official duties, he never ceased to engage in the work he had most at heart—the preaching of Christ. But they were years of stress and conflict. The clouds of religious persecution were again gathering over the land. Soon after the restoration of the dissolute Charles II the persecution began.

James Guthrie, on his way to the martyr's crown, was imprisoned in Edinburgh Castle, together with other protesting ministers. One so prominent as Rutherford was not likely to escape. His work "Lex Rex" was highly obnoxious to Charles and his arbitrary government. It was condemned as a seditious and treasonable book, and publicly burned by the hangman at the cross of Edinburgh, and later under the windows of Rutherford's College at St. Andrews. Rutherford, himself, was deposed from all his offices, and summoned to appear before the next Parliament to answer to the charge of treason.

But the summons came too late. For Rutherford the sands of time were sinking. The messengers found him already on his death-bed. He calmly sent back the message, "I have got a summons already before a superior Judge and judicatory, and I behove to answer my first summons, and ere your day arrive I will be where few Kings and great folks come."

With incredible meanness the enraged Parliament voted that he should not be permitted to die in the College. Lord Burleigh raised a protest: "Ye have voted", said he, "that honest man out of his college, but ye cannot vote him out of heaven."

His preaching finished, and weary of conflict, the dying man turned with longing heart to "Immanuel's high and blessed land" where, as he says, "no wind bloweth but the breathings of the Holy Ghost, no seas nor floods but the pure water of life, that proceedeth from under the throne and from the Lamb! no planting but the Tree of Life that yieldeth twelve manner of fruits every month." When asked, "What think ye now of Christ?" he replied, "I shall live and adore Him. Glory, glory to my Creator and Redeemer for ever. Glory shineth in Immanuel's land." To some brother ministers he said, "My Lord is the chief of ten thousands of thousands. None is comparable to Him, in heaven or on earth. Dear brethren, do all *for Him*. Pray *for Christ*. Preach *for Christ*. Feed the flock committed to your charge *for Christ*. Do all *for Christ*. Beware of men pleasing, there is too much of it. The Chief Shepherd will shortly appear." To one who spoke in praise of his ministry he said, "I disclaim all. The port I would be in at is redemption and forgiveness of sins through His blood."

BIOGRAPHICAL INTRODUCTION

On the last day of his life, March 28, 1661, he said, "This night shall close the door and put my anchor within the veil, and I shall go away in a sleep by five o'clock in the morning." And so it came to pass. At the dawn of the day he answered to the summons from on high, and passed into the presence of his Lord,

Where glory—glory dwelleth
In Immanuel's land.

Hamilton Smith

EXTRACTS FROM THE LETTERS OF SAMUEL RUTHERFORD

1.
The Word of Warning

"Thou hast a name that thou livest, and art dead."

REVELATION 3:1

"I counsel thee to buy of me gold tried in the fire, that thou mayest be rich; and white raiment, that thou mayest be clothed, and that the shame of thy nakedness do not appear; and anoint thine eyes with eyesalve, that thou mayest see."

REVELATION 3:18

TO THE SINNER

Draw by the lap of time's curtain, and look in through the window to great and endless eternity, and consider if a worldly price (suppose this little round clay globe of this ashy and dirty earth, the dying idol of the fools of this world, were all your own) can be given for one smile of Christ's God-like and soul-ravishing countenance. In that day when so many joints and knees of thousand thousands wailing shall stand before Christ, trembling, shouting, and making their prayers to hills and mountains to fall upon them, and hide them from the face of the Lamb, oh, how many would sell lordships and kingdoms that day, and buy Christ! But, oh, the market shall be closed and ended ere then!

Beware of a beguile in the matter of your salvation. Woe, woe for evermore, to them that lose that prize. For what is behind, when the soul is once lost, but that sinners warm their bits of clay houses at a fire of their own kindling, for a day or two (which doth rather suffocate with its smoke than warm them); and at length they lie down in sorrow, and are clothed with everlasting shame! ... O, alas! the greater part of this world run to the place of torment rejoicing and dancing, eating, drinking, and sleeping. ... Fy upon this condemned and foolish world, that would give so little for salvation! Oh, if there were a free market for salvation proclaimed in that day when the trumpet of God shall awake the dead, how many buyers would be then! ... It is a dry and hungry bairn's part of goods that Esaus are hunting for here. I see thousands following the chase, and in the pursuit of such things, while in the meantime they lose the blessing; and, when all is done, they have caught nothing to roast for supper, but lie down hungry. And, besides, they go to bed, when they die, without a candle; for God saith to them, "This ye shall have at My hand, ye shall lie down in sorrow." And truly this is as ill-made a bed to lie upon as one could wish; for he cannot sleep soundly, nor rest sweetly, who hath sorrow for his pillow. ... I am sure that they never got Christ, who were not once sick at the yolk of the heart for Him. Too, too many whole souls think that they have met with Christ, who had never a wearied night for the want of Him: but, alas! what richer are men, that they dreamed the last night they had much gold, and, when they awoke in the morning, they found it was but a dream? What are all the sinners in the world, in that day when heaven and earth shall go up in a flame of fire, but a number of beguiled dreamers? Every one shall say of his hunting and his conquest, "Behold, it was a dream!" Every man in that day will tell his dream. I beseech you, in the

THE WORD OF WARNING

Lord Jesus, beware, beware of unsound work in the matter of your salvation. ... Then after this day, convene all your lovers before your soul, and give them their leave; and strike hands with Christ, that thereafter there may be no happiness to you but Christ, no hunting for anything but Christ, no bed at night, when death cometh, but Christ. Christ, Christ, who but Christ! ... I protest before men and angels that Christ cannot be exchanged, that Christ cannot be sold, that Christ cannot be weighed.

If ye never had a sick night and a pained soul for sin, ye have not yet lighted upon Christ.

No loss is comparable to the loss of the soul; there is no hope of regaining that loss.

To the Professor

All come not home at night who suppose that they have set their face heavenward. It is a woful thing to die, and miss heaven, and to lose house-room with Christ at night: it is an evil journey where travellers are benighted in the fields. I persuade myself that thousands shall be deceived and ashamed of their hope. Because they cast their anchor in sinking sands they must lose it. ... Oh, how many a poor professor's candle is blown out and never lighted again! I see that ordinary profession, and to be ranked amongst the children of God, and to have a name among men, is now thought good enough to carry professors to heaven. But certainly a name is but a name, and will never bide a blast of God's storm. I counsel you not to give your soul or Christ rest, nor your eyes sleep, till ye have gotten something that will abide the fire, and stand out the storm.

Time, custom, and a good opinion of ourselves, our good meaning, and our lazy desires, our fair shows, and the world's glistering lustres, and these broad passments and buskings[1] of religion, that bear bulk in the kirk, is that wherewith most satisfy themselves. But a bed watered with tears, a throat dry with praying, eyes as a fountain of tears for the sins of the land, are rare to be found among us. Oh, if we could know the power of godliness!

I may be a bookman, and yet be an idiot and stark fool in Christ's way! Learning will not beguile Christ. The Bible beguiled the Pharisees, and so may I be misled.

To live as others do, and to be free of open sins that the world crieth shame upon, will not bring you to heaven.

Many are beguiled with this, that they are free of scandalous and crying abominations; but the tree that bringeth forth not good fruit is for the fire. The man that is not born again cannot enter the kingdom of God. Common honesty will not take men to heaven.

Remember, many go far on and reform many things, and can find tears, as Esau did; and suffer hunger for truth, as Judas did; and wish and desire the end of the righteous, as Balaam did; and profess fair, and fight for the Lord, as Saul did; and desire the saints of God to pray for them, as Pharaoh and Simon Magus did; and prophesy and speak of Christ, as Caiaphas did; and walk softly and mourn for fear of judgments, as Ahab did; and put away gross sins and idolatry, as Jehu did; and hear the word of God gladly, and reform their life in many things according to the word, as Herod did; and say to Christ, "Master, I will follow Thee whithersoever Thou goest", as the man who offered to be Christ's servant; and may taste of the virtues of the life to come, and be partaker of the wonderful gifts of the Holy Spirit, and taste of the good word of God, as the apostates who sin against the Holy Ghost. And yet all

---

[1] External decorations.

these are but like gold in clink and colour, and watered brass, and base metal. These are written that we should try ourselves, and not rest till we be a step nearer Christ than sunburnt and withering professors can come.

I see many professors for the fashion, professors of glass; I would make a little knock of persecution, ding[1] them in twenty pieces, and the world would laugh at the shreds. Therefore, make fast work; see that Christ be the ground-stone of your profession. The sore wind and rain will not wash away His building; His work hath no less date than to stand for evermore.

To The Young Man

I must first tell you that there is not such a glassy, icy, and slippery piece of way betwixt you and heaven as Youth; and I have experience to say with me here, and to seal what I assert. The old ashes of the sins of my youth are new fire of sorrow to me. I have seen the devil, as it were, dead and buried, and yet rise again, and be a worse devil than ever he was; therefore, my brother, beware of a green young devil, that hath never been buried. The devil in his flowers (I mean the hot, fiery lusts and passions of youth) is much to be feared: better yoke with an old grey-haired, withered, dry devil. For in youth he findeth dry sticks, and dry coals, and a hot hearthstone; and how soon can he with his flint cast fire, and with his bellows blow it up, and fire the house! Sanctified thoughts, thoughts made conscience of, and called in, and kept in awe, are green fuel that burn not, and are a water for Satan's coal.

There is nothing out of heaven so necessary for you as Christ. And ye cannot be ignorant but your day will end, and the night of death shall call you from the pleasures of this life: and a doom given out in death standeth for ever

---

[1] Knock violently.

—as long as God liveth! Youth, ordinarily, is a post and ready servant for Satan, to run errands; for it is a nest for lust, cursing, drunkenness, blaspheming of God, lying, pride, and vanity. Oh, that there were such an heart in you as to fear the Lord, and to dedicate your soul and body to His service! When the time cometh that your eye-strings shall break, and your face wax pale, and legs and arms tremble, and your breath shall grow cold, and your poor soul look out at your prison house of clay, to be set at liberty; then a good conscience, and your Lord's favour, shall be worth all the world's glory. Seek it as your garland and crown.

It is hardly credible what a nest of dangerous temptations youth is; how inconsiderate, foolish, proud, vain, heady, rash, profane, and careless of God, this piece of your life is; so that the devil findeth in that age a garnished and well-swept house for himself. ... For then affections are on horseback, lofty and stirring; then the old man hath blood, lust, much will, and little wit, and hands, feet, wanton eyes, profane ears, as his servants, and as a king's officers at command, to come and go at his will. Then a green conscience is as supple as the twig of a young tree. It is for every way, every religion; every lewd course prevaileth with it. And, therefore, oh, what a sweet couple, what a glorious yoke, are youth and grace, Christ and a young man! This is a meeting not to be found in every town. None who have been at Christ can bring back ... a report answerable to His worth; for Christ cannot be spoken of, or commended according to His worth. "Come and see", is the most faithful messenger to speak of Him.

Give your will, wit, humour, the green desires of youth's pleasures off your hand to Christ. It is not possible for you to know, till experience teach you, how dangerous a time youth is. It is like green and wet timber. When Christ casteth fire on it, it taketh not fire. There is need here of more than ordinary pains, for corrupt nature hath a good back-friend of youth. And sinning against light will put out your candle, and stupify your conscience, and bring upon it more coverings and skin, and less feeling and sense of guiltiness; and when that is done, the devil is like a mad horse that hath broken his bridle, and runneth away with his rider whither he listeth. Learn to know that which the Apostle knew, the deceitfulness of sin. Strive to make prayer, and reading, and holy company, and holy conference your delight; and when delight cometh in, ye shall by little and little smell the sweetness of Christ, till at length your soul be over head and ears in Christ's sweetness. Then shall ye be taken up to the top of the mountain with the Lord, to know the ravishments of spiritual love, and the glory and excellency of a seen, revealed, felt, and embraced Christ: and then ye shall not be able to loose yourself off Christ, and to bind yourself to old lovers. Then, and never till then, are all the paces, motions, walkings, and wheels of your soul in a right tune, and in a spiritual temper.

TO THE EARTHLY-MINDED

Alas! that the sharp and bitter blasts on face and sides, which meet us in this life, have not learned us mortification, and made us dead to this world! We buy our own sorrow, and we pay dear for it, when we spend out our love, our joy, our desires, our confidence, upon an handful of snow and ice, that time will melt away to nothing, and go thirsty out of the drunken inn when all is done. Alas! that we inquire not for the clear fountain, but are so foolish as to drink foul, muddy, and rotten waters, even till our bedtime. And then in the resurrection, when we shall be awakened, our yesternight's sour drink and swinish dregs shall rift up upon us; and sick, sick shall many a soul be then.

May-flowers, and morning vapour, and summer mist, posteth not so fast away as these worm-eaten pleasures which we follow. We build castles in the air, and night-dreams are our daily idols that we doat on. ... When ye and I shall lie lumps of pale clay upon the ground, our pleasures, that we now naturally love, shall be less than nothing in that day. ... Betake you to Christ without further delay. Ye will be fain at length to seek Him, or do infinitely worse.

This world thinketh heaven but at the next door, and that godliness may sleep in a bed of down till it come to heaven! But that will not do it.

Let not salvation be your by-work or your holy-day's talk only, or a work by the way. For men think this may be done in three days' space on a feather bed, when death and they are fallen in hands together, and that with a word or two they shall make their soul-matters right. Alas! this is to sit loose and unsure in the matters of our salvation. ... Oh, when will men learn to be that heavenly-wise as to divorce from and free their soul of all idol-lovers, and make Christ the only, only One, and trim and make ready their lamps while they have time and day!

2.
The Troubled Soul

> *But flowers need night's cool darkness,*
> *The moonlight and the dew;*
> *So Christ, from one who loved Him,*
> *His shining oft withdrew;*
> *And then for cause of absence,*
> *My troubled soul I scann'd—*
> *But glory, shadeless, shineth*
> *In Immanuel's land.*

"Why art thou cast down, O my soul? and why art thou disquieted within me? hope thou in God: for I shall yet praise Him, who is the health of my countenance, and my God."

PSALM 42:11

THE CLOUDY AND DARK DAY

Believe under a cloud, and wait for Him when there is no moonlight nor starlight. ... Faith's eyes, that can see through a millstone, can see through a gloom of God, and under it read God's thoughts of love and peace. Hold fast Christ in the dark; surely ye shall see the salvation of God.

When Christ hideth Himself, wait on, and make din till He return; it is not time then to be carelessly patient. I love to be grieved when He hideth His smiles. Yet believe

His love in a patient onwaiting and believing in the dark. Ye must learn to swim and hold up your head above the water, even when the sense of His presence is not with you to hold up your chin.

THE HOUR OF TEMPTATION

I find My Lord going and coming seven times a day. His visits are short; but they are both frequent and sweet. ... I hear ill tales, and hard reports of Christ, from the Tempter and my flesh; but love believeth no evil. I may swear that they are liars, and that apprehensions make lies of Christ's honest and unalterable love to me. ... Temptations, that I supposed to be stricken and to be laid upon their backs, rise again and revive upon me; yea, I see that while I live, temptations will not die.

I find it to be most true, that the greatest temptation out of hell is to live without temptations. ... Faith is the better of the free air, and of the sharp winter storm in its face. Grace withereth without adversity. The devil is but God's master fencer, to teach us to handle our weapons.

SELF-OCCUPATION

I am like one travelling in the night, who seeth a spirit, and sweateth for fear, and careth not to tell it to his fellow, for fear of increasing his own fear.

I observe many who think it holiness enough to complain, and set themselves at nothing: as if to say "I am sick" could cure them. They think complaints a good charm for guiltiness.

Let your bleeding soul and your sores be put in the hand of this expert Physician; let young and strong corruption and His free grace be yoked together, and let Christ and your sins deal it betwixt them. I shall be loath to put you off your fears, and your sense of deadness: I wish it were more. There be some wounds of that nature, that their bleeding should not be soon stopped. Ye must take a house beside the Physician. It will be a miracle if ye be the first sick man whom He put away uncured, and worse than He found you. … "Him that cometh unto Me I will in no wise cast out." Take ye that. It cannot be presumption to take that as your own, when you find that your wounds stound[1] you. Presumption is ever whole at the heart, and hath but the truant sickness, and groaneth only for the fashion. Faith hath sense of sickness, and looking to Christ therein, is glad to see a known face. Christ is as full a feast as ye can have to hunger. … He is a miracle and a world's wonder, to a seeking and a weeping sinner; but yet such a miracle as shall be seen by them who will come and see. The seeker and sigher is at last a singer and enjoyer.

Ye complain that ye want a mark of the sound work of grace and love in your soul. For answer, consider for your satisfaction (till God send more) 1 John 3:14. And as for your complaint of deadness and doubtings, Christ will, I hope, take your deadness and you together. They are bodies full of holes … and broken bones which need mending, that Christ the Physician taketh up: whole vessels are not for the Mediator Christ's art. Publicans, sinners, harlots, are ready market-wares for Christ. The only thing that will bring sinners within a cast of Christ's drawing arm is that which ye write of some feeling of death and sin. … A soul bleeding to death, till Christ were sent for, and cried for in all haste, to come and stem the blood, and close up the hole in the wound with His own hand and balm, were a very good disease, when many are dying of a whole heart.

[1] Overpower with pain.

All the truly regenerated cannot determinately tell you the measure of their dejections; because Christ beginneth young with many, and stealeth into their heart, ere they wit of themselves, and becometh homely with them, with little din or noise. I grant that many are blinded, in rejoicing in a good-cheap conversion, that never cost them a sick night. ... But for that; I would say, if other marks be found that Christ is indeed come in, never make plea with Him because He will not answer, "Lord Jesus, how camest Thou in? whether in at door or window?" Make Him welcome, since He is come. "The wind bloweth where it listeth"; all the world's wit cannot perfectly render a reason why the wind should be a month in the east, six weeks possibly in the west, and the space of only an afternoon in the south or north. Ye will not find out all the nicks and steps of Christ's way with a soul, do what ye can; for sometimes He will come in stepping softly, like one walking beside a sleeping person, and slip to the door, and let none know He is there.

Ye challenge yourself that some truths find more credit with you than others. Ye do well; for God is true in the least, as well as in the greatest, and He must be so to you. Ye must not call Him true in the one page of the leaf, and false in the other, for our Lord in all His writings never contradicted Himself yet. Although the best of the regenerate have slipped here, always labour ye to hold your feet.

Ye complain of Christ's short visits, that He will not bear your company one night; but when ye lie down warm at night, ye rise cold at morning. Answer: I cannot blame you (nor any other that knoweth that sweet Guest), to bemoan His withdrawings, and to be most desirous of His abode and company; for He would captivate and engage the affections of any creature that saw His face. Since He looked on me, and gave me a sight of His fair love, He gained my heart wholly, and got away with it. ... He shall keep it long, ere I fetch it from Him. But I shall tell you what ye should do; treat Him well, give Him the chair and the board-head, and make Him welcome to the mean portion ye have. A good supper and kind entertainment maketh guests love the inn the better. Yet sometimes Christ hath an errand elsewhere, for mere trial; and then, though ye give Him King's cheer, He will away; as is clear in desertions for mere trial and not for sin.

I would have written ere now, but people's believing there is in me that which I know there is not, hath put me out of love with writing to any. For it is easy to put religion to a market and public fair; but, alas! it is not so soon made eye-sweet for Christ. My Lord seeth me a tired man, far behind. I have gotten much love from Christ, but I give Him little or none again. My white side cometh out on paper to men; but at home and within I find much black work, and great cause of a low sail, and of little boasting.

3.
The Way of Peace

> *Oh! I am my Belovèd's,*
> *And my Beloved is mine!*
> *He brings a poor vile sinner*
> *Into His "House of wine".*
> *I stand upon His merit,*
> *I know no other stand,*
> *Not e'en where glory dwelleth*
> *In Immanuel's land.*

"By grace are ye saved through faith … not of works."

Ephesians 2:8-9

Free Grace

Grace, grace, free grace, the merits of Christ for nothing, white and fair, and large Saviour-mercy (which is another sort of thing than creature-mercy, or law-mercy, yea, a thousand degrees above angel-mercy), have been, and must be, the rock that we drowned souls must swim to.

I wish all professors to fall in love with grace. All our songs should be of His free grace. We are but too lazy and careless in seeking of it; it is all our riches we have here, and glory in the bud. I wish that I could set out free grace. I was the law's man, and under the law, and under a curse; but grace brought me from under that hard lord, and I rejoice that I am grace's freeholder. I pay tribute to none for heaven, seeing that my land and heritage holdeth of Christ, my new King. Infinite wisdom hath devised this excellent way of freeholding for sinners.

I know no sweeter way to heaven than through free grace and hard trials together; and one of these cannot well want another.

Let us be ballasted with grace, that we be not blown over, and that we stagger not. Yet a little while, and Christ and His redeemed ones shall fill the field, and come out victorious. ... He shall not faint nor be discouraged, till He hath brought forth judgment unto victory.

Faith

Consent and say "Amen" to the promises, and ye have sealed that God is true and Christ is yours. This is an easy market. Ye but look on with faith; for Christ suffered all, and paid all.

When the truth is come to your hand, hold it fast; go not again to make a new search and inquiry for truth. It is easy to cause conscience to believe as ye will, not as ye know.

Christ alone

I am glad to hear that Christ and ye are one, and that ye have made Him your "one thing", whereas many are painfully toiled in seeking many things, and their many things are nothing. It is only best that ye set yourself apart ... for Christ alone; for ye are good for no other thing than Christ; and He hath been going about you these many years, by afflictions, to engage you to Himself. It were a pity and a loss to say Him nay. ... Let us, then, go on to meet with Him, and to be filled with the sweetness of His love. Nothing will hold Him from us. He hath decreed to put time, sin, hell, devils, men, and death out of the way, and to rid the rough way betwixt us and Him, that we may enjoy one another. It is strange and wonderful ... that He would have the company of sinners to solace and delight Himself withal in heaven.

I know that you are looking to Christ and I beseech you to follow your look.

Howbeit this day be not yours and Christ's, the morrow will be yours and His. I would not exchange the joy of my bonds and imprisonment for Christ, with all the joy of this dirty and foul-skinned world.

Make tight work at the bottom, and your ship shall ride against all storms, if withal your anchor be fastened on good ground; I mean within the vail. And verily I think this is all, to gain Christ. All other things are shadows, dreams, fancies, and nothing.

Poor folks must either beg or borrow from the rich; and the only thing that commendeth sinners to Christ is extreme necessity and want. Christ's love is ready to make and provide a ransom, and money for a poor body who hath lost his purse. "Ho, ye that have no money, come and buy" (Isaiah 55:1), that is the poor man's market.

The sweetest and safest course is, for this short time of the afternoon of this old and declining world, to stand for Jesus. He hath said it, and it is our part to believe it, that ere it be long, "Time shall be no more, and the heaven shall wax old, as a garment."

Christ the believer's security

The Nail fastened in a sure place cannot be broken, nor can the smallest vessel fail to find sweet security in dependence upon Him, since all the weight of heaven and earth, of redeemed saints and confirmed angels, is upon His shoulder, I am a fool, and brutish to imagine that I can add anything to Christ's special care of and tenderness to His people. He who keepeth the basins and knives of His house, and bringeth the vessels again to the second temple, must have a more tender care of His redeemed ones than of a spoon, or of Peter's old shoes,[1] which must yet not be lost in his captivity.

Submission

O blessed soul, that could sacrifice his will, and go to heaven, having lost his will and made resignation of it to Christ! I would seek no more than that Christ were absolute King over my will, and that my will were a sufferer in all crosses, without meeting Christ with such a word, "Why is it thus?"

Oh, what wisdom is it to believe, and not to dispute; to subject the thoughts to His court, and not to repine at any act of His justice? He hath done it: all flesh be silent! It is impossible to be submissive and religiously patient, if ye stay your thoughts down among the confused rollings and wheels of second causes; as, "Oh, the place!" "Oh, the time!" "Oh, if this had been, this had not followed!" Oh, the linking of this accident with this time and place! Look up to the master-motion and the first wheel.

Oh, how hard it is to get the intentions so cut off from and raised above the creature, as to be without mixture of creature and carnal interest, and to have the soul, in heavenly actings, only, only eyeing Himself, and acting from love to God, revealed to us in Jesus Christ!

[1] Alluding to Ezra 1:7-11; Acts 12:8.

A GOOD CONSCIENCE

Keep the conscience whole without a crack! If there be a hole in it, so that it take in water at a leak, it will with difficulty mend again. It is a dainty, delicate creature, and a rare piece of the workmanship of your Maker; and therefore deal gently with it, and keep it entire, that amidst this world's glory you may learn to entertain Christ.

4.
The Present Evil World

> *Oh! well it is for ever,*
> *Oh! well for evermore,*
> *My nest hung in no forest*
> *Of all this death-doom'd shore:*
> *Yea, let the vain world vanish,*
> *As from the ship the strand,*
> *While glory—glory dwelleth*
> *In Immanuel's land.*

"The fashion of this world passeth away."

1 CORINTHIANS 7:31

"All that is in the world, the lust of the flesh, and the lust of the eyes, and the pride of life, is not of the Father, but is of the world."—1 JOHN 2:16

Step over this hand-breadth of world's glory into our Lord's new world of grace, and ye will laugh at the feathers that children are chasing in the air. I verily judge that this inn, which men are building their nest in, is not worth a drink of cold water. It is a rainy and smoky house: best we come out of it, lest we be choked with the smoke thereof.

Build your nest upon no tree here; for ye see God hath sold the forest to death; and every tree whereupon we would rest is ready to be cut down, to the end we may fly and mount up, and build upon the Rock. ... There is less sand in your glass now than there was yester-night. This span-length of ever-posting time will soon be ended.

All that is under this vault of heaven, and betwixt us and death, and on this side of sun and moon, is but toys, night-visions, head-fancies, poor shadows, watery froth, godless vanities at their best, and black hearts, and salt and sour miseries, sugared over and confected with an hour's laughter or two, and the conceit of riches, honour, vain, vain court, and lawless pleasures. If ye look both to the laughing side and to the weeping side of this world, and if ye look not only upon the skin and colour of things, but into their inwards, and the heart of their excellency, ye shall see that one look of Christ's sweet and lovely eye, one kiss of His fairest face, is worth ten thousand worlds of such rotten stuff as the foolish sons of men set their hearts upon. ... Turn your heart to the other side of things, and get it once free of these entanglements, to consider eternity. ... As a flood carried back to the sea, so doth the Lord's swift post, Time, carry you and your life with wings to the grave. Ye eat and drink, but time standeth not still; ye laugh, but your day fleeth away; ye sleep, but your hours are reckoned and put by hand. Oh, how soon will time shut you out of the poor, and cold, and hungry inn of this life! And then what will yesterday's short-born pleasures do to you, but be as a snowball melted away many years since? Or worse, for the memory of these pleasures useth to fill the soul with bitterness. Time and experience will prove this to be true; and dying men, if they could speak, would make this good. ... Your love, if it were more than all the love of angels in one, is

Christ's due: other things worthy in themselves, in respect of Christ, are not worth a windlestraw, or a drink of cold water.

I know a man who wondered to see any in this life laugh or sport. Surely our Lord seeketh this of us, as to any rejoicing in present perishing things. ... For I think the men of this world are like children in a dangerous storm in the sea, that play and make sport with the white foam of the waves thereof, coming in to sink and drown them; so are men making fool's sports with the white pleasures of a stormy world, that will sink them. But, alas! what have we to do with their sports which they make? If Solomon said of laughter, that it was madness, what may we say of this world's laughing and sporting themselves with gold and silver, and honours, and court, and broad large conquests, but that they are poor souls, in the height and rage of a fever gone mad? Then a straw, a fig, for all created sports and rejoicing out of Christ! Nay, I think that this world, at its prime and perfection, when it is come to the top of its excellency and to the bloom, might be bought with an half-penny; and that it would scarce weigh the worth of a drink of water. There is nothing better than to esteem it our crucified idol (that is, dead and slain), as Paul did. Then let pleasures be crucified, and riches be crucified, and court and honour be crucified. And since the apostle saith that the world is crucified to him, we may put this world to the hanged man's doom, and to the gallows: and who will give much for a hanged man? as little should we give for a hanged and crucified world. Yet, what a sweet smell hath this dead carrion to many fools in the world! and how many wooers and suitors findeth this hanged carrion! Fools are pulling it off the gallows, and contending for it. Oh, when will we learn to be mortified men, and to have our fill of those things that have but their short summer quarter of this life! If we saw our Father's house, and that great and fair city, the New Jerusalem, which is up above sun and moon, we would cry to be over the water, and to be carried in Christ's arms out of this borrowed prison.

How soon will some few years pass away! and then, when the day is ended, and this life's lease expired, what have men of world's glory but dreams and thoughts?

There will be shortly a proclamation by One standing in the clouds, "that time shall be no more", and that courts with kings of clay shall be no more; and prisons, confinements, forfeitures, wrath of Kings, hazard of lands, houses, and name, for Christ, shall be no more. This world's span-length of time is drawn now to less than half an inch, and to the point of the evening of the day of this old grey-haired world. And, therefore, be fixed and fast for Christ and His truth for a time; and fear not him whose life goeth out at his nostrils, who shall die as a man. ... Kings earthly are but well-favoured little clay-gods, time's idols; but a sight of our invisible King shall decry and darken all the glory of this world. ... All the world shall fall before Him, and (as God liveth!) every arm lifted up to take the crown off His royal head, or that refuseth to hold it on His head, shall be broken from the shoulder blade. Oh, what would men count of clay estates, of time-eaten life, of worm-eaten and moth-eaten worldly glory, in comparison of that fairest ... the Son of the Father's delights!

Look beyond time: things here are but moonshine. They have but children's wit who are delighted with shadows, and deluded with feathers flying in the air.

Verily I have seen the best of this world, a moth-eaten threadbare coat: I propose to lay it aside, being now old and full of holes. O for my house above, not made with hands!

Oh, thrice blinded souls, whose hearts are charmed and bewitched with dreams, shadows, feckless[1] things, night-vanities, and night-fancies of a miserable life of sin! Shame on us who sit still, fettered with the love and liking of a piece of dead clay! Oh, poor fools, who are beguiled with painted things, and this world's fair weather, and smooth promises, and rotten, worm-eaten hopes! May not the devil laugh to see us give out our souls, and get in but corrupt and counterfeit pleasures of sin? O for a sight of eternity's glory, and a little tasting of the Lamb's marriage supper! Half a draught, or a drop of the wine of consolation, that is up at our banqueting-house, out of Christ's own hand, would make our stomachs loathe the brown bread and sour drink of a miserable life. Oh, how far are we bereaved of wit, to chafe, and hunt, and run, till our souls be out of breath, after a condemned happiness of our own making! ... O that we were out of ourselves, and dead to this world, and this world dead and crucified to us! And, when we should be close out of love and conceit of any masked and farded[2] lover whatsoever, then Christ would win and conquer to Himself a lodging in the inmost yolk of our heart. Then Christ should be our night-song and morning-song; and the noise of our Well-beloved's feet, when He cometh, and His first knock ... at the door, should be as news of two heavens to us.

If contentment were here, heaven were not heaven. Whoever seek the world to be their bed, shall at best find it short and ill made, and a stone under their side to hold them waking, rather than a soft pillow to sleep upon. Ye ought to bless your Lord that it is not worse. We live in a

[1] Weak, worthless.
[2] Painted.

sea where many have suffered shipwreck, and have need that Christ sit at the helm of the ship.

I recommend to you holiness and sanctification, and that you keep yourself clean from this present evil world. ... Oh, how hard a thing is it, to get the soul to give up with all things on this side of death and doomsday! We say that we are removing and going from this world; but our heart stirreth not one foot off its seat. Alas! I see few heavenly-minded souls, that have nothing upon the earth but their body of clay going up and down this earth, because their soul and the powers of it are up in heaven, and there their hearts live, desire, enjoy, rejoice. Oh! men's souls have no wings; and, therefore, night and day they keep their nest, and are not acquainted with Christ. ... Take you to your one thing, to Christ, that ye may be acquainted with the taste of His sweetness and excellency; and charge your love not to doat upon this world, for it will not do your business in that day, when nothing will come in good stead to you but God's favour.

Let all the world be nothing, and let God be all things.

5.
The Flesh and the Devil

"Flee also youthful lusts."—2 Timothy 2:22

Lusts

Pride of youth, vanity, lusts, idolizing of the world, and charming pleasures, take long to root them out. ... When the day of visitation cometh, and your old idols come weeping about you, ye will have much ado not to break your heart.

It is impossible that a man can take his lusts to heaven with him; such wares as these will not be welcome there. Oh, how loath are we to forego our packalds and burdens, that hinder us to run our race with patience! It is no small work to displease and anger nature, that we may please God. Oh, if it be hard to win one foot, or half an inch, out of our own will, out of our own wit, out of our own ease and worldly lusts (and so to deny ourself, and to say, "It is not I but Christ, not I but grace, not I but God's glory, not I but God's love constraining me, not I but the Lord's word, not I but Christ's commanding power as King in me!"), oh, what pains, and what a death is it to nature, to turn me, myself, my lust, my ease, my credit, over into, "My Lord, my Saviour, my King, and my God, my Lord's will, my Lord's grace!" But, alas! that idol, that whorish creature, *myself*, is the master-idol we all bow to. … What hurried Eve headlong upon the forbidden fruit, but that wretched thing *herself*? What drew that brother-murderer to kill Abel? That wild *himself*. What drove the old world on to corrupt their ways? Who, but *themselves*, and their own pleasure? What was the cause of Solomon's falling into idolatry and multiplying of strange wives? What, but *himself*, whom he would rather pleasure than God? What was the hook that took David and snared him first in adultery, but his *self-lust?* and then in murder, but his *self-credit* and *self-honour?* What led Peter on to deny his Lord? Was it not a piece of *himself*, and *self-love* to a whole skin? What made Judas sell his Master for thirty pieces of money, but a piece of *self-love*, idolizing of avaricious *self?* What made Demas go off the way of the gospel, to embrace this present world? Even *self-love* and love of gain for himself. Every man blameth the devil for his sins; but the great devil, the house-devil of every man, the house-devil that eateth and lieth in every man's bosom, is that idol that killeth all, *himself*. Oh, blessed are they who can deny themselves, and put Christ in the room of themselves! Oh, would to the Lord that I had not a *myself*, but Christ; nor a *my lust*, but Christ; nor a *my ease*, but Christ; nor a *my honour*, but Christ! O sweet word! "I live no more, but Christ liveth in me!" Oh, if every one would put away himself, his own self, his own ease, his own pleasure, his own credit, and his own twenty things, his own hundred things, which he setteth up, as idols, above Christ!

It is impossible that your idol-sins and ye can go to heaven together; and that they who will not part with these can, indeed, love Christ at the bottom, but only in word and show, which will not do the business.

Contention

I think not much of a cross when all the children of the house weep with me and for me; and to suffer when we enjoy the communion of saints is not much; but it is hard when saints rejoice in the suffering of saints, and redeemed ones hurt (yea, even go nigh to hate) redeemed ones. I confess I imagined there had no more been such an affliction on earth, or in the world, as that one elect angel should fight against another. ... The saints are not Christ: there is no misjudging in Him; there is much in us; and a doubt it is, if we shall have fully one heart till we shall enjoy one heaven. Our star-light hideth us from ourselves and hideth us from one another, and Christ from us all. But He will not be hidden from us. ... The King's spikenard, Christ's perfume, His apples of love, His ointments, even down in this lower house of clay, are a choice heaven. Oh! what then is the King in His own land, where there is such a throne, so many King's palaces, ten thousand thousands of crowns of glory that want heads yet to fill them? Oh, so much leisure as shall be there to sing! Oh, such a tree as groweth there in the midst of that Paradise, where the inhabitants sing eternally under its branches!

Slandering

The times would make any that love the Lord sick and faint, to consider how iniquity aboundeth, and how dull we are in observing sins in ourselves, and how quick-sighted to find them out in others. ... And yet very often, when we complain of times, we are secretly slandering the Lord's work and wise government of the world, and raising a hard report of Him. "He is good, and doeth good", and all His ways are equal. ... Oh, we are little with God! and do all without God! We sleep and wake without Him; we eat, we speak, we journey, we go about worldly business and our calling without God! and, considering what deadness is upon the hearts of many, it were good that some did not pray without God, and preach and praise, and read and confer of God without God! It is universally complained of, that there is a strange deadness upon the land, and on the hearts of His people.

THE DEVIL

Since we must have a devil to trouble us, I love a raging devil best. Our Lord knoweth what sort of devil we have need of: it is best that Satan be in his own skin, and look like himself.

My Lord Jesus had a good eye that the tempter should not play foul play, and blow out Christ's candle. ... When He burnt the house, He saved His own goods. And I believe the devil and the persecuting world shall reap no fruit of me, but burnt ashes: for He will see to His own gold, and save that from being consumed with the fire. ... Oh, what owe I to the file, to the hammer, to the furnace of my Lord Jesus! who hath now let me see how good the wheat of Christ is, that goeth through His mill, and His oven, to be made bread for His own table. Grace tried is better than grace, and it is more than grace; it is glory in its infancy.

Many make a start toward heaven who fall on their back, and win not up to the top of the mount. It plucketh heart and legs from them, and they sit down and give it over, because the devil setteth a sweet-smelled flower to their nose (this fair busked[1] world), wherewith they are bewitched, and so forget or refuse to go forward.

[1] Adorned.

6.
"The Day of Affliction"

I have borne scorn and hatred,
I have borne wrong and shame,
Earth's proud ones have reproach'd me,
For Christ's thrice blessed name:—
Where God His seal set fairest
They've stamp'd their foulest brand;
But judgment shines like noonday
In Immanuel's land.

"In all their affliction He was afflicted."—Isaiah 63:9

"As many as I love, I rebuke and chasten."—Revelation 3:19

AFFLICTION

Know you not that Christ wooeth His wife in the furnace? "Behold I have refined thee, but not with silver; I have chosen thee in the furnace of affliction." He casteth His love on you when you are in the furnace of affliction. You might indeed be casten down if He brought you in and left you there; but when He leadeth you through the waters, think ye not that He has a sweet soft hand? You know His love grip already; you shall be delivered, wait on. Jesus will make a road, and come and fetch home the captive. ... Your winter night is near spent; it is near-hand the dawning. ... This wilderness shall bud and grow up like a rose.

It is good that your crosses will but convoy you to heaven's gates: in, they cannot go; the gates shall be closed upon them, when ye shall be admitted to the throne. Time standeth not still, eternity is hard at our door. Oh, what is laid up for you! therefore, harden your face against the wind.

The thorn is one of the most cursed, and angry, and crabbed weeds that the earth yieldeth, and yet out of it springeth the rose, one of the sweetest-smelled flowers, and most delightful to the eye, that the earth hath. Your Lord shall make joy and gladness out of your afflictions; for all His roses have a fragrant smell. Wait for the time when His own holy hand shall hold them to your nose; and if ye would have present comfort under the cross, be much in prayer, for at that time your faith kisseth Christ and He kisseth the soul.

Every man thinketh he is rich enough in grace, till he take out his purse, and tell his money, and then he findeth his pack but poor and light in the day of a heavy trial. I found that I had not to bear my expenses, and I should have fainted, if want and penury had not chased me to the storehouse of all.

Venture through the thick of all things after Christ, and lose not your Master, Christ, in the throng of this great market. Let Christ know how heavy, and how many a stone-weight you and your cares, burdens, crosses, and sins are. Let Him bear all. ... And then, let the wind blow out of what airt it will, your soul shall not be blown into the sea.

"THE DAY OF AFFLICTION"

Lay all your loads and your weights by faith upon Christ; take ease to yourself, and let Him bear all. ... I rejoice that He hath come, and hath chosen you in the furnace; it was even there where ye and He set tryst. That is an old gate of Christ's: He keepeth the good old fashion with you, that was in Hosea's days: "Therefore, behold, I will allure her, and bring her into the wilderness, and speak to her heart."[1] There was no talking to her heart, while He and she were in the fair and flourishing city, and at ease; but out in the cold, hungry, waste wilderness, He allured her, He whispered news into her ear there, and said, "Thou art Mine."

Wants are my best riches, because I have these supplied by Christ.

We fools would have a cross of our own choosing, and would have our gall and worm-wood sugared, our fire cold, and our death and grave warmed with heat of life; but He who hath brought many children to glory, and lost none, is our best Tutor. I wish that, when I am sick, He may be keeper and comforter. ... But I know it is my softness and weakness, who would ever be ashore when a fit of sea-sickness cometh on; though I know I shall come soon enough to that desirable country, and shall not be displaced: none shall take my lodging.

Your afflictions are not eternal; time will end them, and so shall ye at length see the Lord's salvation. His love sleepeth not, but is still working for you. His salvation will not tarry nor linger; and suffering for Him is the noblest cross that is out of heaven. ... It is a love-look to heaven and the other side of the water that God seeketh; and this is the fruit, the flower and bloom growing out of your cross, that ye be a dead man to time, to clay, to gold, to coun-

---

[1] Hosea 2:14, marginal reading.

try, to friends, wife, children, and all pieces of created things; for in them there is not a seat nor bottom for soul's love. Oh, what room is for your love (if it were as broad as the sea) up in heaven, and in God! And what would not Christ give for your love? God gave so much for your soul; and blessed are ye if ye have a love for Him, and can call in your soul's love from all idols, and can make a God of God, a God of Christ, and draw a line betwixt your heart and Him. ... Let the Lord absolutely have the ordering of your evils and troubles; and put them off you by recommending your cross and your furnace to Him who hath skill to melt His own metal, and knoweth well what to do with His furnace. Let your heart be willing that God's fire have your tin, and brass, and dross. ... When ye are over the water, this case shall be a yesterday past a hundred years ere ye were born; and the cup of glory shall wash the memory of all this away, and make it as nothing. ... The Lord is rising up to do you good in the latter end; put on the faith of His salvation, and see Him posting and hasting towards you.

If your Lord call you to suffering, be not dismayed; there shall be a new allowance of the King for you when you come to it. One of the softest pillows Christ hath is laid under His witnesses' head, though often they must set down their bare feet among thorns.

SUFFERING AND REPROACH

Christ is pleased to feast a poor prisoner, and to refresh me with joy unspeakable and glorious! so as the Holy Spirit is witness that my sufferings are for Christ's truth. ... Now, I testify under my hand, out of some small experience, that Christ's cause, even with the cross, is better than the king's crown; and that His reproaches are sweet, His cross perfumed, the walls of my prison fair and large, my losses gain.

"THE DAY OF AFFLICTION"

I beseech you therefore, in the bowels of Jesus, set before your eyes the patience of your forerunner Jesus, who, when He was reviled, reviled not again; when He suffered, He threatened not, but committed Himself to Him who judgeth righteously. And since your Lord and Redeemer with patience received many a black stroke on His glorious back, and many a buffet of the unbelieving world, and says of Himself, "I gave My back to the smiters, and My cheeks to them that plucked off the hair; I hid not My face from shame and spitting"; follow Him, and think it not hard that you receive a blow with your Lord. Take part with Jesus of His sufferings and glory in the marks of Christ. ... Be you upon Christ's side, and care not what flesh can do. Hold yourself fast by your Saviour, howbeit you be buffeted, and those that follow Him. Yet a little while and the wicked shall not be. "We are troubled on every side, yet not distressed; we are perplexed, but not in despair; persecuted, but not forsaken; cast down, but not destroyed." If you can possess your soul in patience, their day is coming. ... The way to overcome is by patience, forgiving and praying for your enemies, in doing whereof you heap coals upon their heads, and your Lord shall open a door to you in your troubles. Wait upon Him as the night watch waiteth for the morning. He will not tarry. Go up to your watch-tower, and come not down; but by prayer, and faith, and hope, wait on. When the sea is full, it will ebb again; and so soon as the wicked are come to the top of their pride, and are waxed high and mighty, then is their change approaching. They that believe make not haste.

The worst things of Christ, His reproaches, His cross, are better than Egypt's treasures. He hath opened His door, and taken into His house-of-wine a poor sinner, and hath left me so sick of love for my Lord Jesus, that if heaven were at my disposing, I would give it for Christ, and would not be content to go to heaven, except I were persuaded that Christ were there.

I find that my extremity hath sharpened the edge of His love and kindness, so that He seemeth to devise new ways of expressing the sweetness of His love to my soul. Suffering for Christ is the very element wherein Christ's love liveth, and exerciseth itself. ... And if Christ weeping in sackcloth be so sweet, I cannot find any imaginable thoughts to think what He will be, when we clay-bodies (having put off mortality) shall come up to the marriage-hall and great palace, and behold the King clothed in His royal robes, sitting on His throne. I would desire no more for my heaven beneath the moon, while I am sighing in this house of clay, but daily renewed feasts of love with Christ.

Thanks be to God that you have so learned Christ as to be made a man for Christ of no reputation, for Him. Your despised Master, who made Himself while He was amongst us of no reputation, is now exalted in glory. There is none now to gibe Him by bowing the knee, none now to spit in His face, none now to bring Him under mocking of the purple robe, none to put on His head a crown of thorns. And as you now partake of His sufferings, so shall you hereafter of His glory. You shall sit honourably on thrones; and when the Chief Shepherd appears, you shall receive the crown. I am convinced that it is for conscience toward God that you suffer. The bottom of your testimony and suffering is not so narrow as some think, who study more to decline the cross than to be tender for every truth.

Sickness

Sure I am, it is better to be sick, providing Christ come to the bedside and draw by the curtains, and say, "Courage, I am thy salvation", than to enjoy health, being lusty and strong, and never to be visited of God.

It is a blessed fever that fetcheth Christ to the bedside.

I hear that Christ hath been that kind as to visit you with sickness, and to bring you to the door of the grave; but ye found the door shut (blessed be His glorious name!) while ye be riper for eternity. He will have more service of you. … We have all idol-love, and are inclined to love other things beside our Lord; and, therefore, our Lord hunteth for our love more ways than one or two.

I have heard of your infirmity of body, and sickness. I know the issue shall be mercy to you, and that God's purpose, which lieth hidden underground to you, is to commend the sweetness of His love and care to you from your youth. And if all the sad losses, trials, sicknesses, infirmities, griefs, heaviness, and inconstancy of the creature, be expounded (as sure I am they are) the rods of the jealousy of an Husband in heaven, contending with all your lovers on earth, though there were millions of them, for your love, to fetch more of your love home to heaven, to make it single, unmixed, and chaste, to the Fairest in heaven and earth, to Jesus the Prince of ages, ye will forgive (to borrow that word) every rod of God, and "let not the sun go down on your wrath" against any messenger of your afflicting and correcting Father. … See that the mark at which Christ hath aimed these twenty-four years and above, is, to have the company and fellowship of such a sinful creature in heaven with Him for all eternity; and, because He will not (such is the power of His love) enjoy His Father's glory, and that crown due to Him by eternal generation, without you, by name,[1] therefore believe no evil of Christ: listen to no hard reports that His rods make of Him to you. He hath loved you and washed you from your sins; and what would ye have more? Is that too little except He adjourn all crosses, till ye be where ye shall be out of all capacity, to sigh or be crossed? I hope that ye can desire no more, no greater, nor more excellent suit, than Christ and the fellowship of the Lamb for evermore. And if that desire be answered in heaven (as I am sure it is, and ye cannot deny but it is made sure to you), the want of these poor accidents, of a living husband, of many children, of an healthful body, of a life of ease in the world, without one knot in the rush, are nobly made up, and may be comfortably borne.

WEAKNESS

Oh, how sweet it is for a sinner to put his weakness into Christ's strengthening hand, and to father a sick soul upon such a Physician, and to lay weakness before Him to weep upon Him, and to plead and pray! Weakness can speak and cry, when we have not a tongue. "And when I passed by thee, and saw thee polluted in thy own blood, I said unto thee, when thou wast in thy blood, Live." ... As for weakness, we have it that we may employ Christ's strength because of our weakness.

I should succumb and come short of heaven, if I had no more than my own strength to support me; and if Christ should say to me, "Either do or die", it were easy to determine what should become of me. ... Christ is kindest in His love, when we are at our weakest; and if Christ had not been to the fore, in our sad days, the waters had gone over our soul. His mercy hath a set period, and appointed place, how far and no farther the sea of affliction shall

---

[1] Alluding to John 10:3, 16; 17:24.

flow, and where the waves thereof shall be stayed. He prescribeth how much pain and sorrow, both for weight and measure we must have. Ye have, then, good cause to recall your love from all lovers, and give it to Christ. He who is afflicted in all your afflictions, looketh not on you in your sad hours with an insensible heart or dry eyes.

Chastening

Ye are His Wheat, growing in our Lord's field; and if wheat, ye must go under our Lord's threshing-instrument, in His barn-floor, and through His sieve,[1] and through His mill to be bruised … that ye may be found good bread in your Lord's house. … I am persuaded your glass is spending itself by little and little; and if ye knew who is before you, ye would rejoice in your tribulations. Think ye it a small honour to stand before the throne of God and the Lamb? and to be clothed in white, and to be called to the marriage supper of the Lamb? and to be led to the fountain of living waters, and to come to the Well-head, even God Himself, and get your fill of the clear, cold, sweet, refreshing water of life, the King's own well? … Up your heart! shout for joy! Your King is coming to fetch you to His Father's house.

Oh thrice fools are we, who, like new-born princes weeping in the cradle, know not that there is a kingdom before them! Then let our Lord's sweet hand square us and hammer us, and strike off the knots of pride, self-love, and world-worship, and infidelity, that He may make us stones and pillars in His Father's house.

It is the Lord's kindness that He will take the scum off us in the fire. Who knoweth how needful winnowing is to us, and what dross we must want ere we enter into the kingdom of God? So narrow is the entry to heaven, that

---

[1] Alluding to Amos 9:9; Luke 22:31.

our knots, our bunches and lumps of pride, and self-love, and idol-love, and world-love, must be hammered off us, that we may thring[1] in, stooping low, and creeping through that narrow and thorny entry.

On this side of the New Jerusalem, we shall still have need of forgiving and healing grace. I find crosses of Christ's carved work that He marketh out for us, and that with crosses He figureth and portrayeth us to His own image, cutting away pieces of our ill and corruption. Lord cut, Lord carve, Lord wound, Lord do anything that may perfect Thy image in us, and make us meet for glory.

[1] Press.

7.
"The Fiery Trial"

> *Deep waters cross'd life's pathway,*
> *The hedge of thorns was sharp;*
> *Now these lie all behind me—*
> *Oh! for a well-tuned harp!*
> *Oh! to join Halleluiah*
> *With yon triumphant band,*
> *Who sing, where glory dwelleth,*
> *In Immanuel's land.*

"When thou passest through the waters, I will be with thee … when thou walkest through the fire, thou shalt not be burned."

ISAIAH 43:2

Who knoweth the truth of grace without a trial? Oh, how little getteth Christ of us, but that which He winneth (to speak so) with much toil and pains! And how soon would faith freeze without a cross!

Learn to make your evils your great good; and to spin comforts, peace, joy, communion with Christ, out of your troubles, which are Christ's wooers, sent to speak for you to Himself.

I find it hard work to believe when the course of providence goeth crosswise to our faith, and when misted souls in a dark night cannot know east by west, and our sea-compass seemeth to fail us. Every man is a believer in daylight: a fair day seemeth to be made all of faith and hope. What a trial of gold is it to smoke it a little above the fire! but to keep gold perfectly yellow-coloured amidst the flames, and to be turned from vessel to vessel, and yet to cause our furnace to sound and speak, and cry the praises of the Lord, is another matter.

I bless the Lord, that all our troubles come through Christ's fingers, and that He casteth sugar among them, and casteth in some ounce-weights of heaven, and of the Spirit of glory that resteth on suffering believers, into our cup, in which there is no taste of hell.

Losses and disgraces are the wheels of Christ's triumphant chariot. In the sufferings of His own saints, as He intendeth their good, so He intendeth His own glory. ... We creep in under our Lord's wings in the great shower, and the water cannot come through those wings. ... We may sing ... even in our winter storm, in the expectation of a summer sun, at the turn of the year. No created powers in hell, or out of hell, can mar the music of our Lord Jesus, nor spoil our song of joy. Let us then be glad, and rejoice in the salvation of our Lord; for faith had never yet cause to have wet cheeks, and hanging-down brows, or to droop or die.

Losses, disappointments, ill-tongues, loss of friends, houses, or country, are God's workmen, set on work to work good to you, out of everything that befalleth to you. Let not the Lord's dealing seem harsh, rough, or unfatherly, because it is unpleasant. When the Lord's blessed will bloweth across your desires, it is best, in humility, to

"THE FIERY TRIAL"

strike sail to Him, and to be willing to be led any way our Lord pleaseth. ... Ye know not what the Lord is working out of this, but ye shall know it hereafter.

I am taught in this ill weather to go on the lee-side of Christ, and to put Him in between me and the storm; and (I thank God) I walk on the sunny side of the brae.

We take ill with it, and can hardly endure to set our paper-face to one of Christ's storms, and to go to heaven with wet feet, and pain, and sorrow. We love to carry a heaven to heaven with us, and would have two summers in one year, and no less than two heavens. But this will not do for us: one (and such a one) may suffice us well enough. The man, Christ, got but one only, and shall we have two?

I am like an old crazed ship that hath endured many storms, and that would fain be in the lee of the shore, and feareth new storms; I would be that nigh heaven, that the shadow of it might break the force of the storm, and the crazed ship might win to land. My Lord's sun casteth a heat of love and beam of light on my soul.

I see grace groweth best in the winter. ... I shall think it mercy to my soul, if my faith shall out-watch all this winter-night, and not nod nor slumber till my Lord's summer-day dawn upon me. ... God be thanked that Christ in His children can endure a stress and a storm, howbeit soft nature would fall down in pieces.

Christ's enemies are but breaking their own heads in pieces, upon the rock laid in Zion; and the stone is not removed out of its place. Faith hath cause to take courage from our very afflictions; the devil is but a whetstone to sharpen the faith and patience of the saints. I know that he but heweth and polisheth stones, all this time for the new Jerusalem.

They are not worthy of Jesus who will not take a blow for their Master's sake.

If ye were not strangers here, the dogs of the world would not bark at you. You may see all windings and turnings that are in your way to heaven out of God's Word; for He will not lead you to the kingdom at the nearest, but you must go through "honour and dishonour, by evil report and good report; as deceivers, and yet true; as unknown and yet well known; as dying, and behold, we live; as chastened, and not killed; as sorrowful, and yet always rejoicing." The world is one of the enemies we have to fight with, but a vanquished and overcome enemy, and like a beaten and forlorn soldier; for our Jesus hath taken the armour from it. Let me, then, speak to you in His words: "Be of good courage," saith the Captain of our salvation, "for I have overcome the world." You shall neither be free of the scourge of the tongue, nor of disgraces (even if it were buffetings and spittings upon the face, as was our Saviour's case), if you follow Jesus Christ. I beseech you in the bowels of our Lord Jesus, keep a good conscience, as I trust you do. You live not upon men's opinion; gold may be gold, and have the King's stamp upon it, when it is trampled upon by men. Happy are you, if, when the world trampleth upon you in your credit and good name, yet you are the Lord's gold, stamped with the King of heaven's image, and sealed by the Spirit unto the day of your redemption. Pray for the spirit of love; for "love beareth all things, it believeth all things, hopeth all things, and endureth all things."

Be not afraid of men. Your Master can mow down His enemies, and make withered hay of fair flowers. Your time will not be long; after your afternoon will come your evening, and after evening night. Serve Christ. ... Let His cause be your cause; give not an hair-breadth of truth away; for it is not yours, but God's. Then, since ye are going, take Christ's testificate with you out of this life—"Well done, good and faithful servant!" His "well done" is worth a shipful of "good-days" and earthly honours.

I never knew, by my nine years' preaching, so much of Christ's love, as He has taught me by six months' imprisonment.

Oh, what art is it to learn to endure hardness, and to learn to go barefooted either through the devil's fiery coals, or his frozen waters!

Think it not strange that men devise against you; whether it be to exile, the earth is the Lord's; or perpetual imprisonment, the Lord is your light and liberty; or a violent and public death, for the kingdom of heaven consisteth in a fair company of glorified martyrs and witnesses; of whom Jesus Christ is the chief witness, who for that cause was born and came into the world. Happy are ye if ye give testimony to the world of your preferring Jesus Christ to all powers.

Fear not men, for the Lord is your light and salvation. It is true, it is somewhat sad and comfortless that ye are your lone; but so it was with our precious Master: nor are ye your lone, for the Father is with you.

Think it not strange, beloved in our Lord Jesus, that Satan can command keys of prisons, and bolts, and chains. This is a piece of the devil's princedom that he hath over the world. Interpret and understand our Lord well in this. Be not jealous of His love, though He make devils and men His under-servants to scour the rust off your faith, and purge you from your dross. And let me charge you, O prisoners of hope, to open your window, and to look out by faith, and behold heaven's post (that speedy and swift salvation of God), that is coming to you. It is a broad river that faith will not look over: it is a mighty and a broad sea, that they of a lively hope cannot behold the furthest bank and other shore thereof. Look over the water; your anchor is fixed within the vail; the one end of the cable is about the prisoner of Christ, and the other end is entered within the vail, whither the Forerunner is entered for you. It can go straight through the flames of the fire of the wrath of men, devils, losses, tortures, death, and not a thread of it be singed or burnt: men and devils have no teeth to bite it in two. Hold fast till He come. ... Enjoy your Beloved, and dwell upon His love, till eternity come in time's room, and possess you of your eternal happiness. Keep your love to Christ, lay up your faith in heaven's keeping, and follow the Chief of the house of the martyrs that witnessed a fair confession before Pontius Pilate. Your cause and His is all one. ... Laugh ye at the giddy-headed clay pots, and stout, brain-sick worms, that dare say in good earnest, "This man shall not reign over us!" as though they were casting the dice for Christ's crown, which of them should have it. I know that ye believe the coming of Christ's kingdom; and that there is a hole out of your prison, through which ye see daylight.

My shallow and ebb thoughts are not the compass which Christ saileth by. I leave His ways to Himself, for they are far, far above me: only I would contend with Christ for His love, and be bold to make a plea with Jesus, my Lord, for a heart-fill of His love; for there is no more left to me. What standeth beyond the far end of my sufferings, and what shall be the event, He knoweth, and I hope, to my joy, will make me know, when God will unfold His decrees concerning me. For there are windings, and to's and fro's, in His ways, which blind bodies like us cannot see.

"THE FIERY TRIAL"

Your time is measured, and your days and hours of suffering from eternity were, by infinite wisdom, considered.

I seek no more, next to heaven, than that He may be glorified in a prisoner of Christ; and that in my behalf many would praise His high and glorious name who heareth the sighing of the prisoner.

8.
The Shadow of Death

I shall sleep sound in Jesus,
 Fill'd with His likeness rise
To live and to adore Him,
To see Him with these eyes.
'Tween me and resurrection
But Paradise doth stand;
Then—then for glory dwelling
In Immanuel's land!

"Though I walk through the valley of the shadow of death, I will fear no evil: for Thou art with me."—Psalm 23:4

"There shall be no more death."—Revelation 21:4

Though I was lately knocking at death's gate, yet I could not get in, but was sent back for a time. It is well if I could yet do any service for Him.

If death which is before you ... were any other thing than a friendly dissolution, and a change, not a destruction of life, it would seem a hard voyage to go through such a sad and dark trance, so thorny a valley, as is the wages of sin. But I am confident the way you know, though your foot never trod in that black shadow. The loss of life is gain to you. If Christ Jesus be the period, the end, and lodging-home, at the end of your journey, there is no fear; ye go to a Friend. And since you have had communion with Him in this life ... ye may look death in the face with joy.

If, in that last journey, ye tread on a serpent in the way, and thereby wound your heel, as Jesus Christ did before you, the print of the wound shall not be known at the resurrection of the just. Death is but an awesome step, over time and sin, to sweet Jesus Christ who knew and felt the worst of death, for death's teeth hurt Him. We know death hath no teeth now, no jaws, for they are broken. It is a free prison; citizens pay nothing for the grave. The jailor who had the power of death is destroyed: praise and glory be to the First-begotten of the dead.

I fear the clay house is a-taking down and undermining: but it is nigh the dawning. Look to the east, the dawning of the glory is near. Your Guide is good company, and knoweth all the miles, and the ups and downs in the way. The nearer the morning, the darker. Some travellers see the city twenty miles off, and at a distance; and yet within the eighth part of a mile they cannot see it.

The way ye know; the passage is free and not stopped; the print of the footsteps of the Forerunner is clear and manifest; many have gone before you. Ye will not sleep long in the dust before the Daybreak.

Remember, how swiftly God's post time flieth away; and that your forenoon is already spent, your afternoon will come, and then your evening, and at last night, when ye cannot see to work. Let your heart be set upon finishing of your journey, and summing and laying your accounts with your Lord. Oh how blessed shall ye be to have a joyful welcome of your Lord at night!

I doubt not but in death ye shall see all things more distinctly, and that then the world shall bear no more bulk than it is worth, and that then it shall couch and be contracted into nothing; and ye shall see Christ longer, higher, broader, and deeper than ever He was. O blessed conquest, to lose all things, and to gain Christ!

Oh, how sweet and comfortable will the feast of a good conscience be to you, when your eye-strings shall break, your face wax pale, and the breath turn cold, and your poor soul come sighing to the windows of the house of clay of your dying body, and shall long to be out, and to have the jailor to open the door, that the prisoner may be set at liberty! … set your heart on the inheritance. Go up beforehand and see your lodging. Look through all your Father's rooms in heaven: in your Father's house are many dwelling-places. Men take a sight of lands ere they buy them. I know that Christ hath made the bargain already; but be kind to the house ye are going to, and see it often. Set your heart on things that are above, where Christ is at the right hand of God.

Your life hath been near the grave, and you were at the door, and you found the door shut and fast: your dear Christ thinking it not time to open these gates to you till you have fought some longer in His camp. And therefore He willeth you to put on your armour again, and to take no truce with the devil or this present world. You are little obliged to any of the two: but I rejoice in this, that when any of the two comes to suit your soul in marriage, you have an answer in readiness to tell them: "You are too long a-coming; I have many a year since promised my soul to another, even to my Lord Jesus, to whom I must be true."

9.
The House of Mourning

> *Soon shall the cup of glory*
> *Wash down earth's bitterest woes,*
> *Soon shall the desert-briar*
> *Break into Eden's rose:*
> *The curse shall change to blessing—*
> *The name on earth that's bann'd,*
> *Be graven on the white stone*
> *In Immanuel's land.*

"The ransomed of the Lord ... shall obtain joy and gladness, and sorrow and sighing shall flee away."—Isaiah 35:10

"God shall wipe away all tears from their eyes; and there shall be no more death, neither sorrow, nor crying."

Revelation 21:4

The loss of a child

Faith will teach you to kiss a striking Lord; and so acknowledge the sovereignty of God (in the death of a child) to be above the power of us mortal men, who may pluck up a flower in the bud and not be blamed for it. If our dear Lord pluck up one of His roses, and pull down sour and green fruit before harvest, who can challenge Him? For He sendeth us to His world, as men to a market, wherein some stay many hours, and eat and drink, and buy and sell, and pass through the fair, till they be weary; and such are those who live long, and get a heavy fill of this life. And others again come slipping in to the morning market, and do neither sit nor stand, nor buy nor sell, but look about them a little, and pass presently home again; and these are infants and young ones, who end their short market in the morning, and get but a short view of the fair. Our Lord, who hath numbered man's months, and set him bounds that he cannot pass, hath written the length of our market, and it is easier to complain of the decree than to change it.

Believe that he is not gone away, but sent before; and that the change of the country should make you think, that he is not lost to you who is found to Christ, and that he is now before you; and that the dead in Christ shall rise again. A going-down star is not annihilated, but shall appear again. If he hath casten his bloom and flower, the bloom is fallen in heaven, into Christ's lap. And as he was lent a while to time, so he is given now to eternity, which will take yourself. The difference of your shipping and his to heaven and Christ's shore, the land of life, is only in some few years, which weareth every day shorter; and some short and soon-reckoned summers will give you a meeting with him. ... If death were a sleep that had no wakening, we might sorrow. ... He breweth your cup: therefore, drink it patiently and with the better will. Stay and wait on, till Christ loose the knot that fasteneth His cross on your back; for He is coming to deliver. And I pray you, learn to be worthy of His pains who correcteth. And let Him wring and be ye washen; for He hath a Father's heart, and a Father's hand, who is training you up, and making you meet for the high hall. This school of suffering is a preparation for the King's higher house; and let all your visitations speak all the letters of your Lord's summons. They cry—"O vain world!" "O bitter sin!" "O short and uncertain time!" "O fair eternity that is above sickness of death!" "O kingly and princely Bridegroom, hasten glory's marriage, shorten time's short-spun and soon-broken thread, and conquer sin!" ... And the Spirit and the Bride say, "Come!" and answer ye with them, "Even so, come, Lord Jesus! come quickly!"

THE LOSS OF A DAUGHTER

Think her not absent who is in such a friend's house. Is she lost to you who is found to Christ? If she were with a dear friend, although you should never see her again, your care for her would be but small. Oh, now, is she not with a dear Friend? and gone higher, upon a certain hope that ye shall, in the Resurrection, see her again. ... You would be sorry either to be, or to be esteemed, an atheist; and yet, not I, but the Apostle, thinketh those to be hopeless atheists who mourn excessively for the dead. ... Follow her, but envy her not; for indeed it is self-love in us that maketh us mourn for them that die in the Lord. Take heed, then, that in showing your affection in mourning for your daughter, ye be not, out of self-affection mourning for yourself. ... Your daughter is plucked out of the fire, and she resteth from her labours; and your Lord, in that, is trying you, and casteth you in the fire. Go through all fire to your rest. ... While ye prodigally spend time in mourning for her, ye are speedingly posting after her. Run with patience your race. Let God have His own; and ask of Him, instead of your daughter which He hath taken from you, the daughter of faith, which is patience; and in patience possess your soul. Lift up your head: ye do not know how near your redemption doth draw.

As I have heard of the death of your daughter with heaviness of mind on your behalf, so am I much comforted that she hath evidenced to yourself and other witnesses the hope of the resurrection of the dead. ... Though we cannot outrun nor overtake them that are gone before, yet we shall quickly follow them; and the difference is, that she hath the advantage of some months or years of the crown before you and her mother. As we do not take it ill if our children outrun us in the life of grace, why then are we sad if they outstrip us in the attainment of the life of glory? It would seem that there is more reason to grieve that children live behind us, than that they are glorified and die before us. All the difference is in some poor hungry accidents of time, less or more, sooner or later. ... Ye would have lent her to glorify the Lord upon earth, and He hath borrowed her (with promise to restore her again) to be an organ of the immediate glorifying of Himself in heaven. Sinless glorifying of God is better than sinful glorifying of Him.

The loss of a son

Dearest brother, go on and faint not. Something of yours is in heaven, beside ... your exalted Saviour; and ye go on after your own. Time's thread is shorter by one inch than it was. I make bold, in Christ, to speak my poor thoughts to you concerning your son lately fallen asleep in the Lord. ... I know that grace rooteth not out the affections of a mother, but putteth them upon His wheel who maketh all things new, that they may be refined: therefore, sorrow for a dead child is allowed to you, though by measure and ounce-weights. ... He commandeth you to weep: and that princely One, who took up to heaven with Him a man's heart to be a compassionate High Priest, became your fellow and companion on earth by weeping for the dead. ... The cup ye drink was at the lip of Jesus, and He drank of it; ... and I conceive ye love it not the worse that it is thus sugared. Therefore, drink, and believe the resurrection of your son's body. ... The good Husbandman may pluck His roses, and gather His lilies at midsummer, and, for aught I dare say, in the beginning of the first summer month; and He may transplant young trees out of the lower ground to the higher, where they may have more of the sun, and a more free air, at any season of the year. What is that to you or me? The goods are His own. The Creator of time and winds did a merciful injury (if I dare borrow the word) to nature, in landing the passenger so early. They love the sea too well who complain of a fair wind, and a desirable tide, and a speedy coming ashore in that land where all the inhabitants have everlasting joy upon their heads.

Violent death is a sharer with Christ in His death, which was violent. It maketh not much what way we go to heaven: the happy home is all, where the roughness of the way shall be forgotten. He is gone home to a Friend's house, and made welcome, and the race is ended: time is recompensed with eternity, and copper with gold.

THE LOSS OF A MOTHER

It hath seemed good, as I hear, to Him that hath appointed the bounds for the number of our months, to gather in a sheaf of ripe corn, in the death of your Christian mother, into His garner. It is the more evident that winter is near, when apples, without the violence of wind, fall of their own accord off the tree. She is now above the winter, with a little change of place, not of a Saviour; only she enjoyeth Him now without messages, and in His own immediate presence, from whom she heard by letters and messengers before. I grant that death is to her a very new thing; but heaven was prepared of old. And Christ (as enjoyed in His highest throne, and as loaded with glory, and incomparably exalted above men and angels ...) is to her a new thing, but so new as the first summer-rose, or the first fruits of that heavenly field; or as a new paradise to a traveller, broken and worn out of breath with the sad occurrences of a long and dirty way. ... It cost her no more to go thither, than to suffer death to do her this piece of service: for by Him who was dead, and is alive, she was delivered from the second death. What, then, is the first death to the second? Not a scratch of the skin of a finger to the endless second death. And now she sitteth for eternity in a very considerable land, which hath more than four summers in the year. Oh, what spring-time is there! ... What a singing life is there! There is not a dumb bird in all that large field; but all sing and breathe out heaven, joy, glory, dominion to the high Prince of that new-found land. And, verily, the Land is the sweeter that Jesus Christ paid so dear a rent for it. And He is the glory of the land: all which, I hope, doth not so much mitigate and allay your grief for her part (though truly this should seem sufficient), as the unerring expectation of the dawning of that day upon yourself, and the hope that you have of the fruition of that same King and kingdom to your own soul.

THE LOSS OF A WIFE

If the place she hath left were any other than a prison of sin, and the home she is gone to any other than where her Head and Saviour is King of the land, your grief had been more rational. But I trust your faith of the resurrection of the dead in Christ to glory and immortality, will lead you to suspend your longing for her, till the morning and dawning of that day when the archangel shall descend with a shout, to gather all the prisoners out of the grave, up to Himself. To believe this is best for you; and to be silent, because He hath done it, is your wisdom.

THE HOUSE OF MOURNING

THE LOSS OF A HUSBAND

It hath pleased the Lord to remove your husband soon to his rest; but shall we be sorry that our loss is his gain, seeing his Lord would want[1] his company no longer? Think not much of short summons; for, seeing he walked with his Lord in his life, and desired that Christ should be magnified in him at his death, ye ought to be silent and satisfied. ... Know that the wounds of your Lord Jesus are the wounds of a lover, and that He will have compassion upon a sad-hearted servant; and that Christ hath said, He will have the husband's room in your heart. He loved you in your first husband's time, and He is but wooing you still. Give Him heart and chair, house and all. He will not be made companion with any other. Love is full of jealousies: He will have all your love; and who should get it but He? I know that ye allow it upon Him. There are comforts both sweet and satisfying laid up for you: wait on.

---

[1] To be deprived of.

10.
The Word of Comfort

With mercy and with judgment
 My web of time He wove,
And aye the dews of sorrow
 Were lustred with His love.
I'll bless the hand that guided,
 I'll bless the heart that plann'd,
When throned where glory dwelleth
 In Immanuel's land.

"A word in season to him that is weary."—Isaiah 50:4

Courage! up your heart! When ye do tire, He will bear both you and your burden. Yet a little while and ye shall see the salvation of God.

Ye cannot, ye must not, have a more pleasant or more easy condition here, than He had, who through afflictions was made perfect. We may indeed think, Cannot God bring us to heaven with ease and prosperity? Who doubteth but He can? But His infinite wisdom thinketh and decreeth the contrary; and we cannot see a reason for it, yet He hath a most just reason. We never with our eyes saw our own soul; yet we have a soul. We see many rivers, but we know not their first spring and original fountain; yet they have a beginning. ... When ye are come to the other side of the water, and have set down your foot on the shore of glorious eternity, and look back again to the waters and to your wearisome journey, and shall see, in that clear glass of endless glory, nearer to the bottom of God's wisdom, ye shall then be forced to say, "If God had done otherwise with me than He hath done, I had never come to the enjoying of this crown of glory." ... Whether God come to His children with a rod or a crown, if He come Himself with it, it is well. Welcome, welcome, Jesus, what way soever Thou come, if we can get a sight of Thee.

Till He take His children out of the furnace that knoweth how long they should be tried, there is no deliverance; but after God's highest and fullest tide, that the sea of trouble is gone over the souls of His children, then comes the gracious long-hoped-for ebbing and drying up of the waters. ... Do not faint; the wicked may hold the bitter cup to your head, but God mixeth it, and there is no poison in it. They strike, but God moves the rod; Shimei curseth, but it is because the Lord bids him.

Ere it be long, our Master will be at us, and bring this whole world out, before the sun and daylight, in their blacks and whites. Happy are they who are found watching. Our sand glass is not so long as we need to weary; time will eat away and root out our woes and sorrow. Our heaven is in the bud, and growing up to an harvest. Why, then, should we not follow on, seeing that our span-length of time will come to an inch? Therefore I commend Christ to you, as the staff of your old age. Let Him now have the rest of your days. And think not much of a storm upon the ship that Christ saileth in: there shall no passenger fall over board, but the crazed ship and the sea-sick passenger shall come to land safe.

I long to know how matters stand betwixt Christ and your soul. I know that ye find Him still the longer the better: time cannot change Him in His love. Ye may yourself ebb and flow, rise and fall, wax and wane; but your Lord is this day as He was yesterday. And it is your comfort that your salvation is not rolled upon wheels of your own making, neither have ye to do with a Christ of your own shaping. God hath singled out a Mediator strong and mighty: if ye and your burdens were as heavy as ten hills or hells, He is able to bear you, and save you to the uttermost. Your often seeking to Him cannot make you a burden to Him. I know that Christ compassionateth you, and maketh a moan for you, in all your dumps, and under your down-castings; but it is good for you that He hideth Himself sometimes. It is not niceness, dryness, nor coldness of love, that causeth Christ to withdraw, that ye cannot see Him; but He knoweth that ye could not bear with upsails, a fair gale, a full moon, and a high spring-tide of His felt love, and always a fair summer-day and a summer-sun of a felt and possessed and embracing Lord Jesus. ... He could not let out His rivers of love upon His own, but these rivers would be in hazard of loosening a young plant at the root. ... Ye should, therefore, frist[1] Christ's kindness, as to its sensible and full manifestations, till ye and He be above sun and moon. That is the country where ye will be enlarged for that love which ye dow[2] not now contain. ... Lighten your heart by laying your all upon Him.

Faint not, because this world and ye are at yea and nay, and because this is not a home that laugheth upon you. The wise Lord, who knoweth you, will have it so, because He casteth a net for your love, to catch it and gather it in to Himself. Therefore, bear patiently the loss of children,

[1] To put off for a time.
[2] Can.

and burdens, and other discontentments, either within or without the house: your Lord in them is seeking you, and seek ye Him. Let none be your love and choice, and the flower of your delights, but your Lord Jesus. Set not your heart upon the world, since God hath not made it your portion; for it will not fall to you to get two portions, and to rejoice twice, and to be happy twice, and to have an upper heaven, and an under heaven too.

Weary not, but come in and see if there be not more in Christ than the tongue of men and angels can express. If ye seek a gate to heaven, the way is in Him, or He is it. What ye want is treasured up in Jesus; and He saith, all His are yours.

Your life is hid with Christ in God, and therefore ye cannot be robbed of it. Our Lord handleth us, as fathers do their young children; they lay up jewels in a place, above the reach of the short arms of bairns, else bairns would put up their hands and take them down, and lose them soon. So hath our Lord done with our spiritual life. Jesus Christ is the high coffer in the which our Lord hath hid our life; we children are not able to reach up our arm so high as to take down that life and lose it; it is in our Christ's hand. ... So long as this life is not hurt, all other troubles are but touches in the heel.

Let us not weary: the miles to that land are fewer and shorter than when we first believed. Strangers are not wise to quarrel with their host, and complain of their lodging. It is a foul way but a fair home. ... The hope of it in the end is a heartsome convoy in the way.

There is a rest for the people of God. Christ possesseth it now one thousand six hundred years before many of His members; but it weareth not out.

The saints know not the length and largeness of the sweet earnest, and of the sweet green sheaves before the harvest, that might be had on this side of the water, if we would take more pains. ... We all go to heaven with less earnest, and lighter purses of the hoped-for sum, than otherwise we might do, if we took more pains to win further in upon Christ, in this pilgrimage of our absence from Him.

Oh that every hair of my head, and every member and every bone in my body, were a man to witness a fair confession for Him! I would think all too little for Him. When I look over beyond the line, and beyond death, to the laughing side of the world, I triumph, and ride upon the high places of Jacob; howbeit otherwise I am faint, dead-hearted, cowardly man, oft borne down, and hungry in waiting for the marriage supper of the Lamb. Nevertheless, I think it the Lord's wise love that feeds us with hunger, and makes us fat with wants and desertions.

We are fallen in winnowing and trying times. I am glad that your breath serveth you to run to the end, in the same condition and way wherein ye have walked these twenty years past. It is either the way of peace, or we are yet in our sins, and have missed the way. The Lord, it is true, hath stained the pride of all our glory; and now, last of all, the sun hath gone down upon many of the prophets. But stumble not; men are but men, and God appeareth more and more to be God, and Christ is still Christ. ... A stronger than I am had almost stumbled me and cast me down. But oh what mercy is it to discern between what is Christ's and what is man's, and what way the hue, colour, and lustre of gifts of grace dazzle and deceive our weak eyes! Oh to be dead to all things that are below Christ, were it even a created heaven and created grace! Holiness is not Christ; nor are the blossoms and flowers of the Tree of Life the tree itself. Men and creatures may wind themselves between us and Christ; and, therefore, the Lord hath done much to take out of the way all betwixt Him and us. ... The fairest things, and most eminent in Britain, are stained, and have lost their lustre; only, only Christ keepeth His greenness and beauty, and remaineth what He was. Oh, if He were more and more excellent to our apprehensions than ever He was (whose excellency is above all apprehensions), and still more and more sweet to our taste! I care for nothing, if so be that I were nearer to Him. And yet He fleeth not from me: I flee from Him, but He pursueth.

The scarcity of faith in the earth saith, "We are hard upon the last nick of time": blessed are those who keep their garments clean against the Bridegroom's coming.

Make you ready to meet the Lord; and rest and sleep in the love of that Fairest among the sons of men. Desire Christ's beauty. Give out all your love to Him, and let none fall by. Learn in prayer to speak to Him.

The Lord hath told you what ye should be doing till He come. "Wait and hasten," saith Peter, "for the coming of our Lord." All is night that is here, in respect of ignorance and daily ensuing troubles, one always making way to another, as the ninth wave of the sea to the tenth; therefore sigh and long for the dawning of that morning, and the breaking of that day of the coming of the Son of Man, when the shadows shall flee away. Persuade yourself the King is coming; read His letter sent before Him, "Behold, I come quickly." Wait with the wearied night-watch for the breaking of the eastern sky, and think that ye have not a morrow. As the wise father said, who, being invited against to-morrow to dine with his friend, answered, "These many days I have had no morrow at all."

11.
The Pilgrim

> *I have wrestled on towards Heaven,*
>   *'Gainst storm, and wind, and tide:—*
> *Now, like a weary traveller,*
>   *That leaneth on his guide,*
> *Amid the shades of evening,*
>   *While sinks life's ling'ring sand,*
> *I hail the glory dawning*
>   *From Immanuel's land.*

"I am a stranger in the earth."—PSALM 119:19

I persuade myself that this world is to you an unco[1] inn; and that ye are like a traveller, who hath his bundle upon his back, and his staff in his hand, and his feet upon the door-threshold. Go forward, in the strength of your Lord (let the world bide at home and keep the house), with your face toward Him, who longeth more for a sight of you than ye can do for Him. Ere it be long He will see us. I hope to see you laugh as cheerfully after noon, as ye have mourned before noon. The hand of the Lord, the hand of the Lord be with you in your journey. What have ye to do

---

[1] Strange.

here? This is not your mountain of rest. Arise, then, and set your foot up the mountain; go up out of the wilderness, leaning upon the shoulder of your Beloved. If ye knew the welcome that abideth you when ye come home, ye would hasten your pace; for ye shall see your Lord put up His own holy hand to your face, and wipe all tears from your eyes; and I trow, then ye shall have some joy at heart.

Be not cast down in heart to hear that the world barketh at Christ's strangers; they do it because their Lord hath chosen them out of this world. And this is one of our Lord's reproaches, to be hated and ill-entreated by men. The stranger, in an uncouth country, must take with a smoky inn and coarse cheer, a hard bed, and a barking ill-tongued host. It is not long to the day, and he will to his journey upon the morrow, and leave them all. Indeed, our fair morning is at hand, the day-star is near the rising, and we are not many miles from home. What matters ill entertainment in the smoky inns of this miserable life? We are not to stay here, and we will be dearly welcome to Him whom we go to. … When I shall see you clothed in white raiment, washed in the blood of the Lamb, … and a crown upon your head, and following our Lamb and lovely Lord whithersoever He goeth,—you will think nothing of all these days; and you shall then rejoice, and no man will take your joy from you. It is certain there is not much sand to run in your Lord's sand-glass, and that day is at hand; and till then your Lord in this life is giving you some little feasts. It is true you see Him not now as you shall see Him then. Your well-beloved standeth now behind the wall looking out at the window, and you see but a little of His face. Then, you shall see all His face and all the Saviour, the loveliest person among the children of men. … You will have cause to hold up your heart in remembrance and hope of that fair, long summer-day. ... Remember you are in the body, and it is the lodging-house: and you may not, without offending the Lord, suffer the old walls of that house to fall down through want of necessary food. Your body is the dwelling-house of the Spirit; and therefore, for the love you carry to the sweet Guest, give a due regard to His house of clay. When He looseth the wall, why not? Welcome, Lord Jesus! But it is a fearful sin in us, by hurting the body by fasting, to loose one stone or the least piece of timber in it, for the house is not your own.

Make others to see Christ in you, moving, doing, speaking, and thinking. Your actions will smell of Him if He be in you. There is an instinct in the new-born babes of Christ, like the instinct of nature that leads birds to build their nests, and bring forth their young, and love such and such places, as woods, forests, and wildernesses, better than other places. The instinct of nature maketh a man love his mother-country above all countries; the instinct of renewed nature, and supernatural grace, will lead to such and such works, as to love your country above, to sigh to be clothed with your house not made with hands, and to call your borrowed prison here below a borrowed prison, and to look upon it servant-like and pilgrim-like.

The sea-sick passenger shall come to land; Christ will be the first to meet you on the shore. ... Keep the King's highway. Go on (in the strength of the Lord), in haste, as if ye had not leisure to speak to the innkeepers by the way. He is over beyond time, on the other side of the water, who thinketh long for you.

I am, in this house of pilgrimage, every way in good case: Christ is most kind and loving to my soul. It pleaseth Him to feast, with His unseen consolations, a stranger and an exiled prisoner; and I would not exchange my Lord Jesus with all the comfort out of heaven.

Sit far back from the walls of this pest-house, even the pollutions of this defiling world. Keep your taste, your love, and hope in heaven; it is not good that your love and your Lord should be in two sundry countries. Up, after your lover, that ye and He may be together. A King from heaven hath sent for you: by faith He showeth you the New Jerusalem, and taketh you alongst in the Spirit, through all the ease-rooms and dwelling-houses in heaven, and saith, "All these are thine; this palace is for thee and Christ." ... Take with you in your journey what you may carry with you, your conscience, faith, hope, patience, meekness, goodness, brotherly kindness; for such wares as these are of great price in the high and new country whither ye go. As for other things, which are but the world's vanity and trash, since they are but the house-sweepings, ye will do best not to carry them with you. Ye found them here; leave them here, and let them keep the house. ... Fasten your grips fast upon Christ. ... I rejoice that He is in heaven before me. God send a joyful meeting; and, in the meantime, the traveller's charges for the way, I mean a burden of Christ's love, to sweeten the journey, and to encourage a breathless runner; for when I lose breath, climbing up the mountain, He maketh new breath.

It is not a smooth and easy way, neither will your weather be fair and pleasant; but whosoever hath seen the invisible God, and the fair City, makes no reckoning of losses and crosses.

A borrowed lodging and some years' house-room, and bread and water, and fire, and bed and candle, are all a part of the pension of my King and Lord; to whom I owe thanks, and not to a creature. I thank God that God is God, and Christ is Christ, and the earth the earth, and the devil the devil, and the world the world, and that sin is sin, and that everything is what it is; because He hath taught me in my wilderness not to shuffle my Lord Jesus, nor to intermix Him with creature-vanities, nor to spin or twine Christ or His sweet love in one web, or in one thread, with the world and the things thereof. Oh, if I could hold and keep Christ all alone, and mix Him with nothing! ... But we are still ill scholars, and will go in at heaven's gates wanting the half of our lesson; and shall still be bairns, so long as we are under time's hands, and till eternity cause a sun to arise in our souls that shall give us wit.

It were now a desirable life to send away our love to heaven. And well it becometh us to wait for our appointed change, yet so as we should be meditating thus: "Is there a new world above the sun and moon? And is there such a blessed company harping and singing hallelujahs to the Lamb up above? Why, then, are we taken with a vain life of sighing and sinning? Oh, where is our wisdom, that we sit still, laughing, eating, sleeping prisoners, and do not pack up all our best things for the journey, desiring always to be clothed with our house from above, not made with hands!" Ah! we savour not the things that are above, nor do we smell of glory ere we come thither; but we transact and agree with time, for a new lease of clay mansions. Behold, He cometh!

It is a good country we are going to, and there is ill lodging in this smoky house of the world, in which we are yet living. ... My counsel is, that ye come out and leave the multitude, and let Christ have your company. Let them take clay and this present world who love it. Christ is a more worthy and noble portion: blessed are those who get Him.

12.
The Eternal Weight of Glory

The sands of time are sinking,
 The dawn of Heaven breaks,
The summer morn I've sighed for,
 The fair sweet morn awakes:
Dark, dark hath been the midnight,
 But dayspring is at hand,
And glory—glory dwelleth
 In Immanuel's land.

"The sufferings of this present time are not worthy to be compared with the glory which shall be revealed in us."

ROMANS 8:18

Oh happy soul for evermore, who can rightly compare this life with that long-lasting life to come, and can balance the weighty glory of the one with the light golden vanity of the other!

When we shall come home, and when our heads shall find the weight of the eternal crown of glory, and when we shall look back to pains and sufferings, then shall we see life and sorrow to be less than one step or stride from a prison to glory; and that our little inch of time-suffering is not worthy of our first night's welcome-home to heaven.

If ye would lay the price ye give out (which is but some few years' pain and trouble) beside the commodities ye are to receive, ye would see they are not worthy to be laid in the balance together: but it is nature that maketh you look what ye give out, and weakness of faith that hindereth you to see what ye shall take in. ... Think ye much to follow the heir of the crown, who had experience of sorrows, and was acquainted with grief? It were pride to aim to be above the King's Son: it is more than we deserve, that we are equals in glory, in a manner.

There hath not been so much taken from your time of ease and created joys, as eternity shall add to your heaven. Ye know that when one day in heaven hath paid you (yea, and overpaid your blood, bonds, sorrow, and sufferings), that it would trouble angels' understanding to lay the count of that surplus of glory which eternity can and will give you. Oh but your sand-glass of sufferings and losses cometh to little, when it shall be counted and compared with the glory that abideth you on the other side of the water! ... If your mind could fancy as many created heavens as time hath had minutes, trees have had leaves, and clouds have had raindrops, since the first stone of the creation was laid, they should not make half a scale in which to bear and weigh boundless excellency. And, therefore, the King whose marks ye are bearing, and whose dying ye carry about with you in your body, is, out of all cry and consideration, beyond and above all our thoughts.

Since ye have not now many years to your endless eternity, and know not how soon the sky above your head will rive, and the Son of Man will be seen in the clouds of heaven, what better and wiser course can ye take, than to think that your one foot is here, and your other foot in the life to come, and to leave off loving, desiring, or grieving for the wants that shall be made up when your Lord and ye shall meet. ... Ye shall then rejoice with joy unspeakable and full of glory, and your joy shall none take from you. It is enough, that the Lord hath promised you great things, only let the time of bestowing them be in His own carving. It is not for us to set an hour-glass to the Creator of time.

When your Head shall appear, your Bridegroom and Lord, your day shall than dawn, and it shall never have an afternoon, nor an evening shadow.

Ye cannot be too often awakened to go forward towards your city, since your way is long, and (for anything ye know) your day is short. And your Lord requireth of you, as ye advance in years and steal forward insensibly towards eternity, that your faith may grow and ripen for the Lord's harvest. For the great Husbandman giveth a season to His fruits that they may come to maturity, and having gotten their fill of the tree they may be then shaken and gathered in for use; whereas the wicked rot upon the tree, and their branch shall not be green. "He shall shake off his unripe grape as the vine, and shall cast off his flower as the olive." It is God's mercy to you, that He giveth you your fill, even to loathing, of this bitter world, that ye may willingly leave it. And at last, having trampled under feet all the rotten pleasures that are under sun and moon, and having rejoiced as though ye rejoiced not, and having bought as though ye possessed not, ye may arrive at our Lord's harbour, and be made welcome, as one of those who have ever had one foot loose from the earth, longing for that place where your soul shall feast and banquet for ever and ever, ... and where ye shall see the fair face of the man Christ, even the beautiful face that was once for your cause more marred than any of the visages of the sons of men, and was all covered with spitting and blood. Be content to wade through the waters betwixt you and glory with Him, holding His hand fast, for He knoweth all the fords. Howbeit ye may be ducked, but ye cannot drown, being in His company. ... Be not afraid, therefore, when ye come even to the black and swelling river of death, to put in your foot and wade after Him. The current, how strong soever, cannot carry you down the water to hell: the Son of God, His death and resurrection, are stepping-stones and a stay to you; set down your feet by faith upon these stones, and go through as on dry land. If ye knew what He is preparing for you, ye would be too glad. He will not (it may be) give you a full draught till you come up to the well-head and drink, yea, drink abundantly, of the pure river of the water of life, that proceedeth out from the throne of God and of the Lamb. Tire not, weary not; when ye are got up thither, and have cast your eyes to view the golden city, and the fair and never-withering Tree of Life, that beareth twelve manner of fruits every month, ye shall then say, "Four-and-twenty hours' abode in this place is worth threescore and ten years' sorrow upon earth."

Oh, if He would fold the heavens together like an old cloak, and shovel time and days out of the way, and make ready in haste the Lamb's wife for her Husband! Since He looked upon me my heart is not my own; He hath run away to heaven with it. ... Look up to Him and love Him. Oh, love and live!

There shall be no complaints on either side, in heaven. There shall be none there, but He and we, the Bridegroom and the bride; devils, temptations, trials, desertions, losses, sad hearts, pain, and death, shall be all put out of play; and the devil must give up his office of tempting. Oh, blessed is the soul whose hope hath a face looking straight out to that day. It is not our part to make a treasure here; anything, under the covering of heaven, which we can build upon, is but ill ground and a sandy foundation. Every good thing, except God, wanteth a bottom, and cannot stand its lone; how then can it bear the weight of us? ... I know that all created power would sink under me, if I should lean down upon it; and, therefore, it is better to rest on God, than to sink or fall; and we weak souls must have a bottom and a being-place, for we cannot stand our lone.

Christ and His cross are not separable in this life; howbeit Christ and His cross part at heaven's door, for there is no house-room for crosses in heaven. One tear, one sigh, one sad heart, one fear, one loss, one thought of trouble, cannot find lodging there: they are but the marks of our Lord Jesus down in this wide inn, and stormy country, on this side of death. Sorrow and the saints are not married together; or, suppose it were so, heaven would make a divorce. I find that His sweet presence eateth out the bitterness of sorrow and suffering. I think it a sweet thing that Christ saith of my cross, "Half mine"; and that He divideth these sufferings with me, and taketh the larger share to Himself; nay, that I and my whole cross are wholly Christ's.

All the saints have their own measure of winter, before their eternal summer. Oh for the long day, and the high sun, and the fair garden, and the King's Great City up above these visible heavens! What God layeth on let us suffer; for some have one cross, some seven, some ten, some half a cross. Yet all the saints have whole and full joy.

I would praise Him for this, that the whole army of the redeemed ones sit rent-free in heaven.

Oh, how sweet to be wholly Christ's, and wholly in Christ! to be out of the creatures owning, and made complete in Christ! to dwell in Immanuel's high and blessed land, and live in that sweetest air where no wind bloweth but the breathings of the Holy Ghost, no seas nor floods flow but the pure water of life, that proceedeth from under the throne and from the Lamb! no planting but the Tree of Life that yieldeth twelve manner of fruits every month! What do we here but sin and suffer? Oh, when shall the night be gone, the shadows flee away, and the morning of that long, long day, without cloud or night dawn? The Spirit and the bride say, "Come." Oh, when shall the Lamb's wife be ready, and the Bridegroom say, "Come!"

Get up in the strength of the Lord; get over the water to possess that good land. It is better than a land of olives and wine-trees; for the Tree of Life, that beareth twelve manner of fruits every month, is there before you; and a pure river of life, clear as crystal, proceeding out of the throne of God and of the Lamb, is there. Your time is short; therefore lose no time. Gracious and faithful is He who hath called you to His kingdom and glory. The city is yours by free conquest, and by promise; and, therefore, let no unco lord-idol put you from your own.

I cannot tell you what is to come. Yet I may speak as our Lord doth of it. The foundation of the city is pure gold, clear as crystal; the twelve ports are set with precious stones; if orchard and rivers commend a soil upon earth, there is a paradise there, wherein groweth the tree of life that beareth twelve manner of fruits every month, which is seven score and four harvests in the year; and there is there a pure river of water of life, proceeding out of the throne of God and of the Lamb; and the city hath no need of the light of the sun or moon, or of a candle, for the

Lord God Almighty and the Lamb is the light thereof. Believe and hope for this, till ye see and enjoy.

13.
The Excellencies of Christ

> *Oh! Christ He is the Fountain,*
> *The deep sweet well of love!*
> *The streams on earth I've tasted,*
> *More deep I'll drink above:*
> *There, to an ocean fulness,*
> *His mercy doth expand,*
> *And glory—glory dwelleth*
> *In Immanuel's land.*

"Whom have I in heaven but Thee? and there is none upon earth that I desire beside Thee."—PSALM 73:25

"What is thy Beloved more than another? ... My Beloved is ... the chiefest among ten thousand. ... He is altogether lovely. This is my Beloved, and this is my friend."

CANTICLES [SONG OF SOLOMON] 5:9-16

CHRIST AND HIS FULNESS

Who knoweth how far it is to the bottom of our Christ's fulness, and to the ground of our heaven? Who ever weighed Christ in a pair of balances? Who hath seen the foldings and plies, and the heights and depths of that glory which is in Him, and kept for us?

He is every way higher, and deeper, and broader than the shallow and ebb handbreadth of my short and dim light can take up; and, therefore, I would that my heart could be silent, and sit down in the learnedly ignorant wondering at the Lord, whom men and angels cannot comprehend. I know that the noonday light of the highest angels, who see Him face to face, seeth not the borders of His infiniteness. They apprehend God near hand; but they cannot comprehend Him. … Oh, let this bit of love of ours, this inch and half-span length of heavenly longing, meet with Thy infinite Love! Oh, if the little I have were swallowed up with the infiniteness of that excellency which is in Christ! … Our wants should soon be swallowed up with His fulness.

Christ and His excellencies

"Come and see" maketh Christ to be known in His excellency and glory. … It is little to see Christ in a book, as men do the world in a card. They talk of Christ by the book and the tongue, and no more; but to come nigh Christ, and hause[1] Him, and embrace Him, is another thing.

Look into those depths (without a bottom) of loveliness, sweetness, beauty, excellency, glory, goodness, grace, and mercy, that are in Christ; and ye shall then cry down the whole world, and all the glory of it, even when it is come to the summer-bloom; and ye shall cry, "Up with Christ, up with Christ's Father, up with eternity of glory!"

Christ and His love

His love hath neither brim nor bottom; His love is like Himself, it passeth all natural understanding. I go to

---

[1] Greet or salute.

fathom it with my arms; but it is as if a child would take the globe of sea and land in his two short arms.

They are happy evermore who are over head and ears in the love of Christ, and know no sickness but love-sickness for Christ, and feel no pain but the pain of an absent and hidden Well-beloved. We run our souls out of breath and tire them, in coursing and galloping after our night-dreams (such are the rovings of our miscarrying hearts), to get some created good thing in this life, and on this side of death. We would fain stay and spin out a heaven to ourselves, on this side of the water; but sorrow, want, changes, crosses, and sin are both woof and warp in that ill-spun web. Oh, how sweet and dear are those thoughts that are still upon the things that are above! and how happy are they who are longing to have little sand in their glass, and to have time's thread cut, and can cry to Christ, "Lord Jesus, have over; come and fetch the dreary passenger!" I wish that our thoughts were more frequently than they are upon our country. Oh, but heaven casteth a sweet smell afar off to those who have spiritual smelling! God hath made many fair flowers; but the fairest of them all is heaven, and the Flower of all flowers is Christ. ... Alas, that there is such a scarcity of love, and of lovers, to Christ amongst us all! Fy, fy, upon us, who love fair things, as fair gold, fair houses, fair lands, fair pleasures, fair honours, and fair persons, and do not pine and melt away with love to Christ! ... If those frothy, fluctuating, and restless hearts of ours would come all about Christ, and look into His love, to bottomless love, to the depth of mercy, to the unsearchable riches of His grace, to inquire after and search into the beauty of God in Christ, they would be swallowed up in the depth and height, length and breadth of His goodness. ... God send me no more, for my part of paradise, but Christ: and surely I were rich enough, and as well heavened as the best of them, if Christ were my heaven.

Hiding of His face is wise love. His love is not fond, doating, and reasonless. ... Nay, His bairns must often have the frosty cold side of the hill, and set down both their bare feet among the thorns. His love hath eyes, and, in the meantime, is looking on. Our pride must have winter weather to rot it. ... The sea-sick passenger shall come to land; Christ will be the first to meet you on the shore. ... Keep the King's highway. Go on (in the strength of the Lord), in haste, as if ye had not leisure to speak to the innkeepers by the way. He is over beyond time, on the other side of the water, who thinketh long for you.

Put Christ's love to the trial, and put upon it our burdens, and then it will appear love indeed. We employ not His love, and therefore we know it not.

Would to God that all cold-blooded, faint-hearted soldiers of Christ would look again to Jesus, and to His love; and when they look, I would have them to look again and again, and fill themselves with beholding of Christ's beauty; and I dare say then that Christ would come into great court and request with many. ... But when I have spoken of Him, till my head rive, I have said just nothing. ... Set ten thousand thousand new-made worlds of angels and elect men, and double them in number, ten thousand, thousand, thousand times; let their heart and tongues be ten thousand thousand times more agile and large, than the heart and tongues of the seraphim that stand with six wings before Him, when they have said all for the glorifying and praising of the Lord Jesus, they have but spoken little or nothing; His love will abide all possible creatures' praise. ... I am confounded with His incomparable love, and that He doth so great things for my soul, and hath got never yet anything of me worth the speaking of.

Running-over love (that vast, huge, boundless love of Christ) is the only thing I most fain would be in hands with. He knoweth that I have little but the love of that love; and that I shall be happy, suppose I never get another heaven but only an eternal, lasting feast of that love. But suppose my wishes were poor, He is not poor: Christ, all the seasons of the year, is dropping sweetness. If I had vessels, I might fill them; but my old, riven, and running-out dish, even when I am at the Well, can bring little away. Nothing but glory will make tight and fast our leaking and rifty vessels.

I want nothing but ways of expressing Christ's love. A full vessel would have a vent. ... Oh! it is a pity that there were not many imprisoned for Christ, were it for no other purpose than to write books and love-songs of the love of Christ. This love would keep all created tongues of men and angels in exercise, and busy night and day to speak of it. Alas! I can speak nothing of it, but wonder at three things in His love: *First*, freedom. O that lumps of sin should get such love for nothing! *Secondly*, the sweetness of His love. I give over either to speak or write of it; but those that feel it, may better bear witness what it is. But it is so sweet, that, next to Christ Himself, nothing can match it. ... And, *thirdly*, what power and strength are in His love! ... it can climb a steep hill; and swim through water and not drown; and sing in the fire and find no pain; and triumph in losses, prisons, sorrows, exile, disgrace, and laugh and rejoice in death. ... Oh, when will we get our day, and heart's fill of that love! ... O time, time! how dost thou torment the souls of those that would be swallowed up of Christ's love, because thou movest so slowly! ... I know it is far after noon, and nigh the marriage-supper of the Lamb; the table is covered already. O Well-beloved, run, run fast! O fair day, when wilt thou dawn! O shadows, flee away!

Oh, that our souls would so fall at odds with the love of this world, as to think of it as a traveller doth of a drink of water, which is not any part of his treasure, but goeth away with the using! for ten miles' journey maketh that drink to him as nothing. Oh, that we had as soon done with this world, and could as quickly dispatch the love of it! But as a child cannot hold two apples in his little hand, but the one putteth the other out of its room, so neither can we be masters and lords of two loves. Blessed were we, if we could make ourselves master of that invaluable treasure, the love of Christ; or rather suffer ourselves to be mastered and subdued to Christ's love, so as Christ were our "all things", and all other things our nothings, and the refuse of our delights.

His love came upon a withered creature, whether I would or not; and yet by coming it procured from me a welcome. A heart of iron, and iron doors, will not hold Christ out. I give Him leave to break iron locks and come in, and that is all.

Keep yourself in the love of Christ, and stand far back from the pollutions of the world.

My prayer to our Lord is, that ye may be sick of love for Him, who died of love for you,—I mean your Saviour Jesus. And O sweet were that sickness to be soul-sick for Him!

Christ, the Same

Jesus, who upon earth ate and drank with publicans and sinners, and spake with harlots, and put up His holy hand and touched the leper's filthy skin, and came evermore nigh sinners, even now in glory, is yet the same Lord. His honour and His great court in heaven hath not made Him forget His poor friends on earth. In Him honours change not manners, and He doth yet desire your company.

Christ—Himself

Our love to Him should begin on earth, as it shall be in heaven; for the bride taketh not, by a thousand degrees, so much delight in her wedding garment as she doth in her bridegroom; so we, in the life to come, howbeit clothed with glory as with a robe, shall not be so much affected with the glory that goeth about us, as with the bridegroom's joyful face and presence.

Love would have the company of the party loved; and my greatest pain is the want of Him, not of His joys and comforts, but of a near union and communion.

Christ beyond compare

Keep your first love with Jesus, fairer than all the children of men. … There is none like Him; I would not exchange one smile of His lovely face with kingdoms. Let others take their silly, feckless heaven in this life. Envy them not; but let your soul, … cast at all things and disdain them, except one only: either Christ or nothing.

I know not a thing worth the buying but heaven; and my own mind is, if comparison were made betwixt Christ and heaven, I would sell heaven with my blessing, and buy Christ.

The saints, at their best, are but strangers to the weight and worth of the incomparable sweetness of Christ.

Oh, what price can be given for Him. Angels cannot weigh Him. Oh, His weight, His worth, His sweetness, His over-passing beauty! If men and angels would come and look to that great and princely One, their ebbness could never take up His depth, their narrowness could never comprehend His breadth, height, and length. If ten thousand worlds of angels were created, they might all tire themselves in wondering at His beauty, and begin again to wonder.

O consider His loveliness and beauty, and that there is nothing which can commend and make fair heaven, or earth, or the creature, that is not in Him in infinite perfection; for fair sun and fair moon are black, and think shame to shine upon His fairness.[1] ... Be homely, and hunger for a feast and fill of His love; for that is the borders and march of heaven. Nothing hath a nearer resemblance to the colour, and hue, and lustre of heaven than Christ loved, and to breathe out love-words and love-sighs for Him. Remember what He is. When twenty thousand millions of heaven's lovers have worn their hearts threadbare of love, all is nothing, yea—less than nothing, to His matchless worth and excellency. Oh, so broad and so deep as the sea of His desirable loveliness is! Glorified spirits, triumphing angels, the crowned and exalted lovers of heaven, stand without His loveliness, and cannot put a circle on it. ... I but spill and lose words in speaking highly of Him who will bide and be above the music and songs of heaven, and never be enough praised by us all.

The discourses of angels, or love-books written by the congregation of seraphim (all their wits being conjoined and melted into one), would for ever be in the nether side of truth, and of plentifully declaring the thing as it is. The infiniteness, the boundlessness of that incomparable excellency that is in Jesus, is a great word.

[1] Alluding to Isaiah 24:23.

If I had as many angels' tongues as there have fallen drops of rain since the creation, or as there are leaves of trees in all the forests of the earth, or stars in the heaven, to praise, yet my Lord Jesus would ever be behind with me.

Put the beauty of ten thousand thousand worlds of paradises, like the garden of Eden, in one; put all trees, all flowers, all smells, all colours, all tastes, all joys, all sweetness, all loveliness, in one: oh, what a fair and excellent thing would that be! And yet it would be less to that fair and dearest Well-beloved Christ, than one drop of rain to the whole seas, rivers, lakes, and fountains of ten thousand earths. Oh, but Christ is heaven's wonder, and earth's wonder! What marvel that His bride saith, "He is altogether lovely!"

> *The Bride eyes not her garment,*
>   *But her dear Bridegroom's face;*
> *I will not gaze at glory,*
>   *But on my King of Grace—*
> *Not at the crown He gifteth,*
>   *But on His piercèd hand:*
> *The **Lamb** is all the glory*
>   *Of Immanuel's land.*